Inter-Organizational Trust in Business-to-Business E-Commerce

Pauline Ratnasingam
University of Vermont, USA

IRM Press
Publisher of innovative scholarly and professional
information technology titles in the cyberage

Hershey • London • Melbourne • Singapore • Beijing

Acquisitions Editor: Mehdi Khosrow-Pour
Senior Managing Editor: Jan Travers
Managing Editor: Amanda Appicello
Development Editor: Michele Rossi
Copy Editor: Ingrid Widitz
Typesetter: Amanda Appicello
Cover Design: Kory Gongloff
Printed at: Integrated Book Technology

Published in the United States of America by
        IRM Press (an imprint of Idea Group Inc.)
        701 E. Chocolate Avenue, Suite 200
        Hershey PA 17033-1117
        Tel: 717-533-8845
        Fax: 717-533-8661
        E-mail: cust@idea-group.com
        Web site: http://www.irm-press.com

and in the United Kingdom by
        IRM Press (an imprint of Idea Group Inc.)
        3 Henrietta Street
        Covent Garden
        London WC2E 8LU
        Tel: 44 20 7240 0856
        Fax: 44 20 7379 3313
        Web site: http://www.eurospan.co.uk

              Library of Congress Cataloging-in-Publication Data

Ratnasingam, Pauline.
   Inter-organizational trust for business to business e-commerce /
Pauline Ratnasingam.
        p. cm.
Available also in electronic form.
Includes bibliographical references and index.
   ISBN 1-931777-75-6 (soft cover) -- ISBN 1-931777-76-4 (ebook)
  1. Electronic commerce--Psychological aspects. 2. Electronic
commerce--Psychological aspects--Case studies. 3. Trust. 4.
Interorganizational relations. I. Title.
   HF5548.32.R378 2003
   658.8'4--dc21
                                                   2002156240

British Cataloguing in Publication Data
A Cataloguing in Publication record for this book is available from the British Library.

New Releases from IRM Press

- **Multimedia and Interactive Digital TV: Managing the Opportunities Created by Digital Convergence**/Margherita Pagani
  ISBN: 1-931777-38-1; eISBN: 1-931777-54-3 / US$59.95 / © 2003
- **Virtual Education: Cases in Learning & Teaching Technologies**/ Fawzi Albalooshi (Ed.), ISBN: 1-931777-39-X; eISBN: 1-931777-55-1 / US$59.95 / © 2003
- **Managing IT in Government, Business & Communities**/Gerry Gingrich (Ed.)
  ISBN: 1-931777-40-3; eISBN: 1-931777-56-X / US$59.95 / © 2003
- **Information Management: Support Systems & Multimedia Technology**/ George Ditsa (Ed.), ISBN: 1-931777-41-1; eISBN: 1-931777-57-8 / US$59.95 / © 2003
- **Managing Globally with Information Technology**/Sherif Kamel (Ed.)
  ISBN: 42-X; eISBN: 1-931777-58-6 / US$59.95 / © 2003
- **Current Security Management & Ethical Issues of Information Technology**/Rasool Azari (Ed.), ISBN: 1-931777-43-8; eISBN: 1-931777-59-4 / US$59.95 / © 2003
- **UML and the Unified Process**/Liliana Favre (Ed.)
  ISBN: 1-931777-44-6; eISBN: 1-931777-60-8 / US$59.95 / © 2003
- **Business Strategies for Information Technology Management**/Kalle Kangas (Ed.)
  ISBN: 1-931777-45-4; eISBN: 1-931777-61-6 / US$59.95 / © 2003
- **Managing E-Commerce and Mobile Computing Technologies**/Julie Mariga (Ed.)
  ISBN: 1-931777-46-2; eISBN: 1-931777-62-4 / US$59.95 / © 2003
- **Effective Databases for Text & Document Management**/Shirley A. Becker (Ed.)
  ISBN: 1-931777-47-0; eISBN: 1-931777-63-2 / US$59.95 / © 2003
- **Technologies & Methodologies for Evaluating Information Technology in Business**/ Charles K. Davis (Ed.), ISBN: 1-931777-48-9; eISBN: 1-931777-64-0 / US$59.95 / © 2003
- **ERP & Data Warehousing in Organizations: Issues and Challenges**/Gerald Grant (Ed.), ISBN: 1-931777-49-7; eISBN: 1-931777-65-9 / US$59.95 / © 2003
- **Practicing Software Engineering in the 21st Century**/Joan Peckham (Ed.)
  ISBN: 1-931777-50-0; eISBN: 1-931777-66-7 / US$59.95 / © 2003
- **Knowledge Management: Current Issues and Challenges**/Elayne Coakes (Ed.)
  ISBN: 1-931777-51-9; eISBN: 1-931777-67-5 / US$59.95 / © 2003
- **Computing Information Technology: The Human Side**/Steven Gordon (Ed.)
  ISBN: 1-931777-52-7; eISBN: 1-931777-68-3 / US$59.95 / © 2003
- **Current Issues in IT Education**/Tanya McGill (Ed.)
  ISBN: 1-931777-53-5; eISBN: 1-931777-69-1 / US$59.95 / © 2003

Excellent additions to your institution's library!
Recommend these titles to your Librarian!

To receive a copy of the IRM Press catalog, please contact
(toll free) 1/800-345-4332, fax 1/717-533-8661,
or visit the IRM Press Online Bookstore at: [http://www.irm press.com]!

Note: All IRM Press books are also available as ebooks on netlibrary.com as well as other ebook sources. Contact Ms. Carrie Skovrinskie at [cskovrinskie@idea-group.com] to receive a complete list of sources where you can obtain ebook information or
IRM Press titles.

Inter-Organizational Trust in Business-to-Business E-Commerce

Table of Contents

Preface

The Internet has revolutionized the capacity to share information across organizations resulting in radical transformations of organizational practices. Most previous research focused on information systems and technology, e-commerce applications such as Inter-Organizational Systems (IOS's), competitive advantages, and security issues, without examining the interactions and behaviors of the trading parties. The emphasis on IOS's gave rise to concerns about Inter-Organizational Relationships (IOR's), as trading partners became aware of the social-political factors that affected their relationships. IOS's involve the sharing of e-commerce applications in different locations. When this study was initiated in 1997, universal standards for business-to-business were not fully developed. This posed a security concern for businesses, in particular Small-Medium-Enterprises (SME's) in Australia and New Zealand. Given the importance of collaborative relations in today's e-business, the role of inter-organizational trust has become of fundamental importance for business-to-business e-commerce. This study aims to examine the importance of inter-organizational trust (or trading partner trust) in e-commerce participation.

Despite the acknowledged importance of trust, only limited research has examined the role of trust among trading partners in business-to-business e-commerce adoption, in which an increased need for trust among trading partners became a salient factor. An exploratory survey together with an in-depth analysis of the literature review provided the theoretical foundations for the development of the conceptual model. Theories from multiple disciplines including marketing, management, sociology, information systems, and e-commerce were applied in the conceptual model. The research question developed for this study was:

How does inter-organizational trust (trading partner trust) influence the perception of e-commerce benefits and risks of e-commerce, thus influencing the extent of e-commerce adoption?

The conceptual model was then tested using a multiple case study research strategy that aimed to solicit qualitative and in-depth understanding of
inter-organizational trust in the context of business-to-business e-commerce.
Eight organizations from a cross-industry selection that formed four bi-directional dyads participated in the study. They included a public sector organization involved in customs clearance; their Internet service provider; a customs
agent (broker); an importer; two organizations in the computer and data communications industry; and two organizations in the telecommunications industry.

The primary unit of analysis in this study is the uni-directional dyad. The
case study participants included e-commerce coordinators, IT managers, security analysts, and senior executives involved in e-commerce operations. In
addition, e-commerce applications, existing documents, and standards contributed to secondary data sources. For example, trading partner agreements,
organizational charts, websites and internal security policies gave evidence of
the organizations' best business practices and background information on the
organizations and their products.

The findings of the four bi-directional dyads (eight organizations) indicated that trust was important for e-commerce adoption. The findings differed
by the type of e-commerce application used and the industry. For example,
organizations that developed extranet applications had only one trading party
(the supplier) undertaking the implementation process. Suppliers were involved
in the installation of their web sites that provided product information. In addition, suppliers had to train their buyers to use extranet applications. The
products consisted of many different parts, (such as data communications,
computers, and telecommunications), which made the task of placing an order
complex. These inter-organizational dyads (Cisco-Compaq NZ and Siemens-
Telecom NZ) experienced relational risks arising from the need to establish
trust among their trading partners. Smaller organizations such as the customs
broker and the importer experienced a smooth e-commerce adoption due to
their application "Trade Manager" which was not connected to the Internet.

The study contributes to theory, practice, and research in the following
ways:

First, rather than inferring characteristics of e-commerce adoption from
a technical and economic background, this study examined behavioural characteristics of trading partners in business-to-business e-commerce from theories in multiple disciplines. The primary emphasis of prior research was on
transaction economics, its competitive advantages, and/or external pressure
(socio-political). This study focused on the importance of inter-organizational
trust in e-commerce adoption. The findings of the study led to the develop-

ment of a model of inter-organizational trust within bi-directional dyads in e-commerce adoption.

Second, the study contributed to practice as it increased the awareness of e-commerce practitioners, who will check the trust behaviours of themselves and those of their trading partners. Trading partners will be better able to select and evaluate technology trust mechanisms in e-commerce, thereby protecting themselves against opportunistic behaviours of their trading partners. Third, the study contributed to research as it paved the way for longitudinal studies. This study only took a micro-perspective of inter-organizational trust within dyadic relationships. Further research should extensively test the model using a field survey with business-to-business e-commerce organizations.

Acknowledgments

While completing a thesis is a solitary task in many ways, the process of writing this book involves many people. First, I would like to thank the members of my dissertation committee for their contribution and support. I would also like to thank the case study participants of the organizations that participated in this study. Finally, I must thank my husband, Mr. Ratnasingam, for the positive encouragement he has given me throughout the years of my study, and my son, Master Denesh, for his patience.

Chapter I

Introduction

In this chapter we introduce the motivation for the study and discuss the background of inter-organizational trust, followed by significant prior research leading to a rationale of this study. Then we discuss previous research in e-commerce adoption, its history, growth, and an analysis of the factors that drive and inhibit e-commerce adoption. E-commerce is the sharing of business information, maintaining business relationships, and conducting business transactions by means of telecommunications networks (Zwass, 1996:3). E-commerce applications facilitate communication and information exchanges between organizations, thereby enabling mass manufacturing, production, and customization to occur (Giaglis et al., 1998). E-commerce is changing the shape of competition, the dynamics of trading partner relationships, and the speed of fulfillment (Kalakota and Robinson, 2001).

In this study, a trading partner is considered to be an organization which engages in business-to-business e-commerce. Trading partners can play various roles of suppliers, merchants, brokers, or customers. They interact with one another to form Inter-organizational relationships (IOR's). To avoid the possibility of anthropomorphizing the organization, and inferring that the trustor is an organization, inter-firm trust is viewed as the collectively held cognitive belief of a group of well-informed individuals within a firm (Zaheer, McEvily, and Perrone, 1998). Thus, in this study the terms *trading partner trust* and *inter-organizational trust* are used interchangeably.

Internet use for business-to-business e-commerce is expected to grow at a spectacular rate. According to Forrester research (2001), the projections for business-to-business e-commerce predict that sales over the Internet will skyrocket to $2.7 trillion by the year 2004. Network communications over the Internet have offered tremendous market potential for today's e-commerce businesses (Applegate et al., 1996; Bakos, 1998; Nath et al., 1998; Kalakota and Robinson, 2001). The benefits of business-to-business e-commerce include global connectivity, high accessibility, scalability, interoperability, and interactivity (Keen, 1999; Nath et al., 1998; Raman, 1996; Turban et al., 2000; Rayport and Jaworski, 2001). The importance of trust in e-business has been widely touted by practitioners and academicians alike (Heil, Bennis, and Stephens, 2000). Even if trust has been traditionally associated with successful buyer-seller relationships (Barney and Hansen, 1994; Bromiley and Cummings, 1995; Doney and Cannon, 1997; Geyskens, Steenkamp, and Kumar, 1998), trust has recently been regarded as the foundation of the digital economy (Keen, 2000).

BACKGROUND OF INTER-ORGANIZATIONAL TRUST IN E-COMMERCE

E-commerce involves the use of computers and telecommunications in routine business relationships. It mostly affects the organizations' operations and daily relationships with their suppliers, customers, banks, insurers, distributors, and other trading partners. The close coupling between buyers and suppliers (sellers) forms inter-organizational relationships. Although most popular accounts of e-commerce focus on business-to-consumer e-commerce, business-to-business e-commerce is becoming key in inter-organizational relationships (Clarke, 1997; Hart and Saunders, 1998; Keen, 2000). Kalakota and Robinson (2001) suggest that virtually every business today is stretched to the limit, while attempting to maintain viability and profitability in the face of unparalleled uncertainty and change. E-commerce introduces an element of additional complexity into inter-organizational relationships (IOR) (Hoffman et al., 1999).

Today's networked economy is notably characterized by the impersonal nature of the online environment and the extensive use of IT, as opposed to face-to-face contact for transactions. The proliferation of advanced e-commerce technologies and the lack of universal standards and policies to guide trading partners have left most organizations adopting e-commerce although lacking the necessary knowledge and expertise to do so. Trading partners do not fully understand the potential use of e-commerce technology and are implementing e-commerce systems for the sole purpose of gaining competitive advantage, without properly considering the trustworthiness of their partners or security consequences (Bensaou and Venkatraman, 1996; Iacovou et al., 1995; Parkhe, 1998; Raman, 1996). Complexity in operating e-commerce applications has led to uncertainties in the e-commerce environment.

The spatial and temporal separation between trading partners by the Internet generates an implicit uncertainty around online transactions (Brynjolfsson and Smith, 2000). The e-business environment is notably characterized by (a) the impersonal nature of the online environment, (b) the extensive use of communication technology as opposed to face-to-face transactions, (c) the implicit uncertainty of using an open technological infrastructure for transactions, and (d) the newness of the transaction medium. Uncertainties inherent in the current e-commerce environment give rise to a lack of trust in e-commerce relationships, thereby creating barriers to trade. For example, Parkhe (1998) and Ring and Van de Ven (1994) identify the following two types of uncertainties. First, uncertainty regarding unknown future events, and secondly, uncertainty regarding trading partners' responses to future events. Uncertainties reduce confidence both in the reliability of business-to-business transactions transmitted electronically and, more importantly, in the trading parties themselves.

On the other hand, trust among trading partners encourages information sharing and opens communication. Interdependencies between organizations arise from sharing e-commerce and associated technologies. Previous research in Electronic Data Interchange (EDI) adoption suggests that these interdependencies can lead to an imbalance of power between smaller suppliers and their more powerful buyers (Hart and Saunders, 1997; Geyskens et al., 1995; Kumar, 1996; Helper, 1991; Webster, 1995). It is in this environment of dual uncertainty that trust becomes important for business-to-business e-commerce.

Research suggests that a perceived lack of trust in e-commerce transactions on the Internet could be a reason for the slow adoption of e-commerce (Keen, 2000; KPMG, 1999; Sabo, 1997; Storresten, 1998). Many businesses perceive that e-commerce transactions are insecure and unreliable.

Despite the assurances of technological security mechanisms (such as encryption and authorization mechanisms, digital signatures, and certification authorities), trading partners in business-to-business e-commerce do not seem to trust the personnel involved in the transactions (CommerceNet, 1997; Fung and Lee, 1999; Marcella et al., 1998; Stewart et al., 2001). Electronic access to information introduces vulnerabilities (such as conflicts, imbalance of power, misleading, and providing inaccurate information from opportunistic behaviours) in inter-organizational relationships. To manage these uncertainties and ensure future opportunities for improving coordination, organizations will need to build trust among their trading partners. According to Keen (1999), trust among trading partners is the currency of e-commerce. He notes "We are moving from an IT economy to a trust economy" (Keen, 1999, p.1). Similarly, O'Hara, Deveraux, and Johansen state that "trust is the glue of global work space and technology does not do much to create relationships" (1994, p. 243-244).

Despite the growth of e-commerce for businesses, only limited research exists that explains how relationships and trust evolve between organizations (Sako, 1998; Smeltzer, 1997).

Significant Prior Research and Research Rationale

The prominence of trust in e-commerce has recently been widely touted by practitioners and academicians alike (Heil, Bennis, and Stephens, 2000; Keen, 2000; Yovovic, 1996). Most of the previous research on trust in business relationships came from the marketing and management literature. Scholars who studied trust in business relationships indicated that high levels of trust help increase competitive advantage, increase satisfaction, develop long-term relationships, reduce risks, and encourage large investments. (See Anderson and Narus, 1994; Barney and Hansen, 1994; Cummings and Bromiley, 1996; Doney and Cannon, 1997; Ganesan, 1994; Geyskens et al., 1998; Hosmer, 1995; Kumar, 1996; Mishra, 1996; Ring and Van de Ven, 1994; Smith and Barclay, 1997; Zaheer et al., 1998.) Despite considerable academic and managerial interest in the issue of trust between trading partners, to date only limited research exists on the determinants of inter-organizational trust (Dyer and Chu, 2000; Sako, 1998; Smeltzer, 1997; Senn, 1998; Zucker, 1986). Zucker (1986, p.59), observed that "for a concept that is acknowledged as central, trust has received very little empirical investigation."

While some scholars (Malone et al., 1987; Clemons et al., 1993) have focused on information technology as a means of reducing inter-organizational transaction costs, the findings of Kumar et al. (1998) suggest the ability to substitute and complement trust and technology in reducing transaction costs in inter-organizational systems (IOS). Similarly, Hart and Saunders (1997), examined power and trust in EDI adoption, and they found that coercive power leads to mistrust, whereas persuasive power is conducive to building trust.

Sydow (1998) defines Inter-organizational trust (IOT) as *"the confidence of an organization in the reliability of other organizations regarding a given set of outcomes or events"* (Sydow, 1998, p.35). As this study examines trust between two organizations (i.e., bi-directional dyads), and since previous research indicates that trust involves risks, we adapt Sydow's definition of trust as our initial definition. Inter-organizational trust in this study is defined as *"the confidence in the reliability of two organizations (bi-directional dyad) in a possibly risky situation, to act competently and dutifully."*

The primary objective of this study is to empirically examine the importance of inter-organizational trust (trading partner trust) in e-commerce adoption. By doing so, trust behaviours in business relationships can be identified. This will, in turn, increase the awareness of e-commerce practitioners, who will then presumably examine their own and their trading partners' trust behaviours. The research question developed for this study is as follows:

> How does inter-organizational trust (trading partner trust) influence the perception of e-commerce benefits and risks of e-commerce, thus influencing the extent of e-commerce adoption?

Previous Research on E-Commerce Adoption

Past researchers who examined e-commerce implementation suggest that e-commerce adoption involves the handling of business transactions over communication networks and may encompass business-to-business, business-to-consumer, and consumer-to-business transactions (Applegate et al., 1996; Kalakota and Robinson, 2001; Senn, 1996; Wigand and Benjamin, 1997). To participate actively in e-commerce, organizations may need to alter their internal and external integration processes and applications. Internal integration could involve interconnection with a variety of applications such as order-entry, invoicing, billing, and payment transfer. External integration includes e-commerce transactions with trading partners, such as suppliers, customers, governmental units, and financial institutions (Iacovou et al., 1995; Heck and Ribbers,

1999). Organizations seeking to participate in e-commerce will need to focus on existing relationships with their trading partners in order to improve their inter-organizational coordination through cooperation and information sharing. Well-documented cases such as Wal-Mart, Levi Strauss, and General Motors describe the creation of new kinds of relationships with certain suppliers and customers through bilateral electronic linkages (Henderson, 1990; Senn, 2000; Zwass, 1999). It is therefore important to note that e-commerce adoption involves both e-commerce technologies and trading partner relationships. The next section discusses the history and growth of e-commerce adoption.

E-COMMERCE HISTORY AND GROWTH

Beginning in the late 1970s, businesses began to conduct a greater portion of their routine buyer-seller operational processes online (Walton, 1997). Although the literature pertaining to Electronic-Data-Interchange (EDI) suggests that significant benefits were achieved by organizations that were using EDI, in reality EDI adoption was not always completely successful. Organizations that used EDI relied mostly on Value-Added-Networks (VAN's) and private messaging networks, both characterized by relatively high costs and limited connectivity. As an automated information exchange, EDI standardizes documents such as purchase orders, invoices, and shipping manifests into agreed open coded format. Connectivity to VAN's was available only for large organizations that relied mostly on mailbox services. VAN's were considered too expensive to implement (Pyle, 1996; Hart and Saunders, 1998). On the other hand, smaller suppliers were pressured to adopt EDI (Barrett, 1999; Helper, 1991; Iacovou et al., 1995; Langfield-Smith and Greenwood, 1998; Webster, 1995).

Over the last several years, organizations have invested heavily in Inter-Organizational-Systems (IOS) and e-commerce applications over the Internet. They include e-mail, Internet-based EDI, extranets, and recently, Web services. What was once cost-effective for only large corporations conducting e-commerce in EDI format is today feasible for all organizations through Internet commerce applications (using Internet-based EDI, intranets, and extranets).

A study conducted by Jupiter Communications indicates the U.S. market for businesses involved in buying and selling goods on the Internet is expected to grow to $6 trillion dollars by 2005, from the current $336 million (New York Times, 2000). This means that in five years (2005), Internet trade will represent

42% of all product buying and selling among businesses, compared to 3% today (in 2000). With such an exponential forecast in the growth of business-to-business e-commerce, establishing trust among trading partners in a global virtual environment becomes crucial.

Factors that Drive E-Commerce Adoption

The Internet and World-Wide-Web are rapidly emerging as an important media for businesses to undertake e-commerce. A number of factors motivate e-commerce participation. They include:

Reduced Costs: Past researchers have noted that the Internet is an inexpensive, flexible, and efficient means for businesses to trade and communicate (Hruska, 1995; Nath et al., 1998; Raman, 1996; Riggins and Rhee, 1998; Senn, 2000; Zwass, 1996). The biggest advantage of Internet-based EDI over VAN is the flat pricing which is not dependent on the volume of information transferred. While EDI conducted via a VAN costs about $150 per hour, the same business conducted over the Internet only costs $1 per hour.

Flexibility: Information on products, prices, business, and services in electronic databases are available to registered trading partners anytime from anywhere in the world. Internet commerce achieves accessibility, availability, and universality because trading partners can interact with one another easily as information and operations take place (Nath et al., 1998; Senn, 2000). Web services enable Internet-based business functions that perform specific business tasks to facilitate business interactions within and beyond the organization.

Open Channels: E-commerce enables business processes and inter-organizational transactions to take place because the Web technology infrastructure performs information storage, browsing, and retrieval needed for these processes and transactions. The interactive capabilities of Web-based electronic catalogs eliminate the need for physical storage and enable dynamic, efficient, and effective updates (Raman, 1996; Shaw, 1997). Prices from different vendors can be compared more easily, thus establishing better communication between suppliers and customers (Cavalli, 1995; Keen, 1999; Nath et al., 1998; Shaw, 1997).

Despite the phenomenal growth in the number of organizations using Internet for e-commerce, some are just not ready to take the plunge (KPMG, 1999). Organizations in a hurry to adopt e-business constantly face technical and operating issues. Some have made mistakes in e-commerce adoption and had to revisit their e-business goals. Many of the strategic issues surrounding the commercialization of the Internet have been clouded in the hype of security and misinformation (Senn, 1998). There are many social, legal, and technological issues at the present level of e-commerce technology which prevent the full realization of its benefits (Caruso, 1995). For example, some organizations are reluctant to publicly admit that they have been subjected to successful attacks by hackers (McWilliams, 2000). It is therefore essential for any e-commerce endeavour to identify the associated threats beforehand and devise a plan to reduce the risks. The next section discusses factors that inhibit e-commerce adoption.

Factors that Inhibit E-Commerce Adoption

Competitive Pressure: Electronic partnerships between buyers and suppliers or manufacturers and distributors have become increasingly inconsistent due to competitive pressures in the global environment that demand quality (Premkumar and Ramamurthy, 1995). Iacovou et al. (1995) suggest that external pressures and organizational readiness may affect e-commerce adoption. For most organizations the biggest challenge is not if or when to consider an Internet commerce solution, but rather how to select the best Internet commerce strategies to develop and sustain competitive advantage. In today's hyper-competitive global marketplace, shareholders and customers are increasingly pressured by businesses to provide easy-to-use, online applications as a better way to conduct business (Premkumar et al., 1997; Keen, 2000).

Pre-Adoption Negotiation: E-commerce adoption, unlike traditional information systems adoption, demands high levels of negotiation, cooperation, and commitment from participating organizations. Selecting transaction sets, negotiating legal matters, and defining performance expectations can burn up hours of staff time and also demand financial and technological resources (Senn, 1998). Furthermore, a survey by Storrosten (1998) revealed that 51% of the respondents cited an internal fear of opening their organization's systems to suppliers, as implementing e-commerce could affect critical business processes such as procurement, inventory management, manufacturing, order fulfillment, shipping, invoicing, payments, and accounting (Nath et al., 1998; Senn, 1998; Storrosten, 1998).

Trust and Security Concerns: Previous studies suggest that businesses have adopted a wait and see attitude toward e-commerce, largely because of security issues (Cavalli, 1995; Norlan and Norton Institute-KPMG, 1999; Ratnasingam, 2001). Other concerns include the expandability of the Internet; and its ability to meet the needs and expectations of all businesses. Even as the Internet becomes more secure, trading partners still do not feel safe. Security is one barrier, but the real underlying factor is insufficient trust in the reliability of Internet-based commerce to absorb the rapid increase in use (Keen, 1999; Raman, 1996). Despite the opportunities of Internet commerce, many businesses are reluctant to go online because they perceive the Internet as an intrinsically insecure environment (Bhimani, 1996; Cavalli, 1995; CommerceNet, 1997; Storrosten, 1998).

Lack of Top Management Support: With poor internal management and a lack of top-level management commitment, implementing e-commerce even with the most advanced products becomes challenging. If management is unwilling to provide adequate financial resources, poor business practices might follow. For example, without full support, an organization might neglect the need for a paper audit trail that would ensure the reliability of electronic certification and business continuity. Successful e-commerce adoption requires full top-level commitment, as many potential adopters are ignorant about the potential and use of e-commerce technologies and their potential benefits and risks (Jamieson, 1996; Marcella et al., 1998; Raman, 1995).

High Costs of Implementing E-Commerce: Start-up costs for implementing e-commerce applications can be high. These include connection costs, hardware, software, set up, and maintenance (Iacovou et al., 1995; Nath et al., 1998; Senn, 1998). Implementation costs may also include conducting an initial search costs, costs of writing contracts, and paying staff to update and maintain electronic databases (Senn, 1998). In addition, contractual, transmission, and coordination costs are also incurred (Nath et al., 1998; Saunders and Clark, 1992).

Technology and infrastructure costs increase as organizations are required to implement compatible systems to receive messages from other trading partners. Organizations need to first develop the necessary IT infrastructure applications, acquire the technical implementation expertise, and invest in training. They must also acquire e-commerce translation and mapping software, and contract with a communication medium or company (Riggins and Mukhopadhyay, 1999). Thus, high costs may create initial barriers to e-commerce participation.

Lack of Standards and Policies: Extranets operate in environments that lack standards and best known practices, which in turn lead to potential compromises in network controls, maintenance, data ownership, internal and external security, and permissions (Riggins and Rhee, 1998; Senn, 1999). Current methods of standardization for structuring data exchanged among extranet applications totally ignore how e-commerce applications were designed to operate. In a survey of the Information Technology American Association (ITAA) industry pulse, Sabo (1997) found that barriers to e-commerce adoption included trust, budget constraints, and public policy regulations. Most organizations do not know what policies to set and many do not even have a complete security policy in place. Lack of consistent government policies, laws, and practices may impact participation in e-commerce.

Lack of Technical Skills, Knowledge, and Expertise: Internet-based e-commerce was in its formative stages in 1997 in Australia and New Zealand when this study was initiated. While the U.S. and Europe were two to three years ahead (Norlan and Norlan, KPMG, 1999). Many trading partners lacked the skills, resources, and technical know-how to implement policies and strategies for secure e-commerce.
Saxena and Wagenaar (1997) conducted a study of EDI adoption at an organizational, industry, and country level. They found that one of the major barriers to successful EDI adoption was limited awareness of promotional activities in EDI use. This line of reasoning was consistent with previous empirical research that suggested that a lack of technical knowledge, expertise, and resources hindered IT use and e-commerce participation (Heck and Ribbers, 1998; Iacovou et al., 1995; Reekers and Smithson, 1996; Saunders and Clark, 1992).

E-Commerce Uncertainties: The proliferation of e-commerce applications have left most trading partners uncertain of e-commerce operations and unaware of the full potential of e-commerce technology (Ghosh, 1998). Uncertainties may arise when trading partners encounter barriers in communication (such as incompatible e-commerce systems, or lack of uniform standards) that may lead to conflicts. Bensaou and Venkatraman (1996) classified three types of vulnerabilities: task, environment, and partnership. Similarly, such matters inside an organization were seen as roadblocks even when EDI was first adopted (Emmelhainz, 1990; Nath et al., 1998; Premkumar et al., 1994). Although risks are inevitable in every trading partner relationships, trust reduces the expectations of opportunistic behavior (Sako and Helper, 1998), and reduces perceptions of risks (Ganesan, 1994).

This chapter laid the foundations for the motivation of this study and introduced the research gap, a research rationale, problem statement, research objective, and research question. Prior significant research together with factors that drive and inhibit e-commerce adoption were presented and discussed. The next chapter discusses the findings of an exploratory survey in e-commerce adoption.

Chapter II

Initial Exploratory Study

In this chapter, we discuss an initial exploratory study conducted via a survey that aimed to examine the extent of e-commerce adoption in Australia and New Zealand. First, the chapter discusses the respondents' profile followed by the key findings that pertained to potential versus achieved benefits, and potential versus perceived barriers and risks. Then we provide a comparison of the findings between Europe and Australia, and New Zealand. Finally, we conclude the chapter with characteristics of e-commerce adopters, namely leaders who have succeeded in e-commerce adoption versus followers who have not, leading to recommendations, lessons learned, and the future of e-commerce in Australia and New Zealand.

An exploratory survey that aimed to examine the extent of e-commerce adoption was mailed out to more than 1,000 Australian and New Zealand organizations. Respondents participating in the survey came from a wide range of organizations operating in Australia and New Zealand. Two hundred and eighty-nine completed questionnaires were received in October 1998 for an initial response rate of 28.9%. However, a number of organizations requested an extension of the survey return deadline via email. Consequently, a second round of the survey was carried out through a secure web site. The extension contributed another twenty responses.

Of the 309 responses, 146 were from Australia, and 163 from New Zealand. The quantitative data set was used for statistical analysis, and comments from respondents led to pattern matching and explanation building.

RESPONDENT PROFILE

E-commerce is said to contribute to a 'death of distance', thereby leading to globalization. First, it is important to assess the geographical reach of the responding organizations. Thirty-five percent of the respondent organizations indicated they had a global reach, while 31% reported a national reach, 21% a regional reach, and 13% a local reach. Second, the nature of industry is likely to affect its propensity for adopting new ways of doing business. The two largest specific industry categories that participated in this survey were the manufacturing/distribution (28%) and the government services (13%).

The pie chart in Figure 1 provides a full breakdown of respondents by industry. Finally, the size of an organization may be an indicator of the resources it can bring to bear on the adoption of a new way of doing business and the level of potential inertia facing the business. The majority of the organizations surveyed (40%) had 100-500 full-time (or equivalent) employees. Nineteen percent had less than 100 employees, 14% had between 500-1000 full-time

Figure 1: Respondent by industry demographics

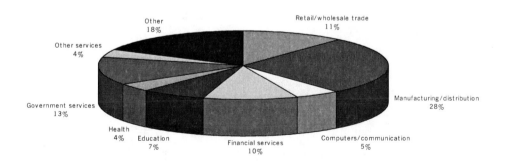

employees, 11% had between 1,000 and 2,000, 9% between 2,000 and 5,000 employees, and 6% had over 5,000 full-time employees.

KEY FINDINGS OF THE EXPLORATORY SURVEY

The findings indicate that organizations within the Asia-Pacific region are beginning to be aware of e-commerce, and for organizations that were brave enough to overcome the perceived and real challenges, this exciting new business tool (that is, the Internet) offers genuine gains in the following ways.

- *Industry Presence*
  The computer and communication industry showed the most aggressive stance and are reaping the greatest gains from electronic commerce. Furthermore, of the 309 companies in Australia and New Zealand surveyed, the educational and financial services sector was also involved in significant adoption of e-commerce technologies.

- *Types of E-Commerce Applications Adopted*
  Four percent of the respondents have implemented smart cards, 6% kiosks, 9% automated teller machine technology, and 16% Interactive Voice Response (IVR). Similarly, only 17% of the respondents are currently implementing certification authority technology.

- *Volume of E-Commerce Transactions*
  In 1997, 1.5 billion electronic transactions occurred in Australia and were worth $16 trillion. In August 1998, there were 21,000 distinct New Zealand organizations connected to the Internet. By the end of 1998, most of the Top 1000 businesses in Australia had an online presence. The largest proportion of respondents (33%) indicated they had between 1,000 and 10,000 electronic transactions per annum. Thirty percent had up to 1,000 transactions per annum, 20% had between 10,000 and 100,000 transactions, 10% had between 100,000 and 500,000 transactions, and 7% had over 500,000 transactions per annum. More than half of the respondents indicated that their transaction value was over one million dollars per annum.

The report emphasized that despite the overall advance, much of the activity related to e-commerce implementation remains in the *'talking stage'*. Most organizations have also realized the importance of implementing e-commerce as in *'must do'* and that whether their adoption will be profitable or not will depend on how they implemented it.

POTENTIAL BENEFITS VS. ACHIEVED BENEFITS

The survey examined respondents' perception of benefits from e-commerce and their assessment of how well they have been able to attain these benefits. As shown in Figure 2, respondents believed that e-commerce was important for improving customer service, improving company's image, optimizing supply chain, and improving productivity, products/service quality, and cost. On the other hand, the data showed that expected benefits from adopting e-commerce technologies and actual benefits achieved have proved somewhat disappointing for many organizations.

E-commerce adoption suggests the importance of *'electronic partnerships'*. In fact, e-commerce, unlike other types of IT innovations, cannot be adopted and used unilaterally. Firms that are motivated to use e-commerce must either find similarly motivated trading partners, or persuade and/or coerce their existing trading partners to adopt e-commerce. This leads to interdependencies between organizations that arise from sharing e-commerce technologies. Moreover, previous research in EDI adoption suggests that these interdependencies led to an imbalance of power between smaller suppliers and their more powerful buyers (Hart and Saunders, 1997; Ratnasingam, 2000). Therefore, this clearly indicates that it is difficult to quantify the costs and benefits in e-commerce usage due to sharing of technologies.

Similarly, much of the failure to *"live up to expectations"* is due to the perception that gains from e-commerce will be easy to achieve. It is assumed that benefits will be achievable within an overly optimistic timeframe that may also be due to inappropriate metrics being applied to measure the success of a venture.

In order to achieve potential benefits, organizations should follow characteristics of leaders that include being smaller and more focused on business benefits in e-commerce. Moreover, organizations should give e-commerce

Figure 2: Potential vs. achieved benefits from e-commerce

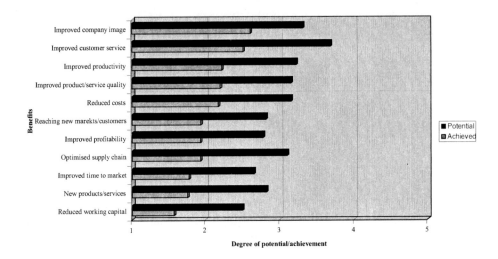

higher importance in their business strategies by having an aggressive cost focus and higher and more specific expectations from technology. Hence, organizations will be able to demonstrate higher levels of integration of e-commerce.

POTENTIAL BARRIERS AND RISKS

Respondents reported the perceived lack of security as one of the main barriers to the adoption of e-commerce technologies, as shown in Figure 3. Based on the findings, this perception was even more remarkable, as solutions for managing security need to be implemented in order to increase e-commerce adoption.

Surprisingly, environmental determinants had little influence on respondents' e-commerce strategic intent. Some of the reasons for the discomfort around security may be explained by ways in which most organizations have developed their key trading partner relationships over time. The highest-ranked element for establishing trust between organizations and their customers and suppliers is the existence of a long history of trading partner trust. This, coupled with a relatively low importance ranking for formal agreements between trading partners as a mechanism for establishing trust, means that organizations have

Figure 3: Potential barriers to adoption of e-commerce

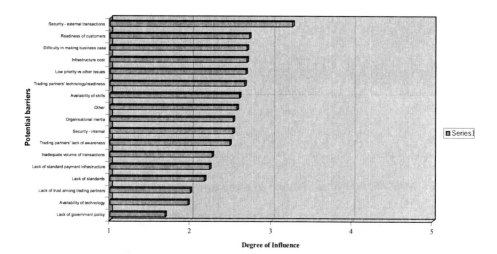

not adjusted to the mindset required to effectively establish trust in electronic trading. It seems that while early adoption of these new business tools in Australia and New Zealand lags behind the United States and Europe, the actual barriers to their widespread acceptance and use are more perceived than real.

In order to overcome these barriers, organizations should choose their trading partners and skills carefully, and start with a need-based strategy rather than a technology based solution, as not all solutions meet the requirements of trading partners. Furthermore, organizations should aim to develop an e-commerce strategy that complements the corporate strategy.

COMPARISONS BETWEEN EUROPE AND AUSTRALIA/NEW ZEALAND (ANZ)

On the security front, the findings claimed that while nearly half (43%) of Australia and New Zealand respondents indicated that security is one of the factors that had a high degree of influence on whether they adopted e-commerce, only 25% of the European respondents in a similar survey indicated that this was a high influence issue (Puchihar et al., 1999). Locally, those still wary about security cited identification and authentication high on the agenda,

Figure 4: Perceived barriers between Europe and ANZ

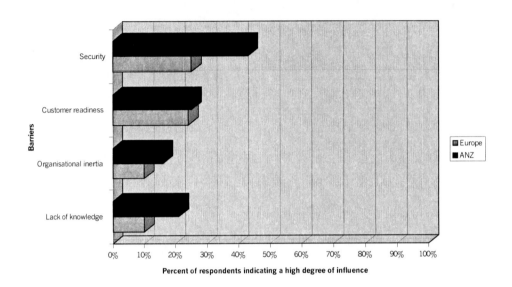

Percent of respondents indicating a high degree of influence

along with the need to implement firewalls. Figure 4 presents a comparison between the findings of Europe and Australia/New Zealand.

Customer readiness falls behind security by one percentage point and is comparable between Europe and Australia/New Zealand. In comparison with European results, Australia/New Zealand still appears to be running security-scared, despite technology solutions being made available and legislation pending.

Of equal concern is the real uncertainty and lack of motivation to implement e-commerce activities. Survey results indicate that organizational inertia is 5% higher in Australia/New Zealand than in Europe, with more than one in five (21%) of the Trans Tasman companies interviewed indicating they felt that they lacked the know-how to implement e-commerce into their businesses.

CHARACTERISTICS OF E-COMMERCE LEADERS

Two groups, known as leaders and followers, were identified from the survey results. They include organizations that have achieved profit or productivity gains from e-commerce implementation and those that have not. The leaders and followers displayed distinct sets of characteristics in terms of e-commerce adoption, implementation, and integration. With regard to e-commerce, 'leaders' are those for whom 'very good' or 'excellent' achievement of profitability and improvement benefits has occurred through e-commerce (or, in the case of non-profit organizations, 'excellent' achievement of productivity and improvement benefits). The following characteristics of leaders help to describe actions that 'followers' might want to take in order to catch up and compete effectively with e-commerce. The leaders' characteristics include:

- Being smaller and more focused on business benefits in e-commerce;

- Being more likely to be in the financial services and computer technology industries;

- Having an aggressive cost focus;

- Giving e-commerce higher importance in their business strategies;

- Having higher and more specific expectations from technology;

- Being less likely to see barriers and better able to minimize those that may exist;

- Demonstrating higher levels of integration of e-commerce across the board;

- Being more likely to have implemented EFT, EDI, Intranet, and Extranet already, and;

- Being far more likely to be conducting marketing, public relations, and advertising via the Internet.

RECOMMENDATIONS AND LESSONS LEARNED

The United States is generally acknowledged as the leader in e-commerce activity, with much of the most aggressive usage and most of the early profitable usage emanating from United States. European constituency is in turn playing catch-up with the United States.

Hence, the critical success factors required for implementing e-commerce can be summarized as follows:

- start with a need-based strategy rather than a technology-based solution, as not all solutions meet requirements and business processes of a trading partner, since some segments will not use the Web;

- develop an e-commerce strategy which complements the corporate strategy;

- aggregate the disparate investments in e-commerce that are likely to be found in any organization;

- avoid layering costs onto the current distribution network and look for substitution between channels;

- choose your trading partners and their skills carefully;

- integrate across the entire organization in order to achieve large efficiency gains;

- a transparent implementation and changing process is important both in terms of acceptance of the change and achieving expected efficiency gains;

- distinguish between striving to win new markets or customers and gaining cost savings from process improvements; and

- develop a benefits register and measure your achievements against it.

THE FUTURE OF E-COMMERCE IN AUSTRALIA AND NEW ZEALAND

The future of e-commerce in Australia and New Zealand looks optimistic, with significant plans being made for increased activity and implementation in the region. The Australian government has acknowledged the opportunities of e-commerce and is working with all Australian states and territories to coordinate efforts to reduce barriers to its adoption. The findings suggest that e-commerce is now reaching a critical mass and, while a number of elements continue to restrict its development, many of these, including the old security scare, are now being overcome.

Significant plans are ahead for implementing e-commerce technologies, and we can expect significant growth in communication technologies, including company web sites, with 22% of respondents indicating they intend to implement web sites within 2000. In the same time frame, 25% intend to implement intranets, 27% extranets, 20% firewalls, 19% Electronic Data Interchange (EDI), and 15% certification/digital signatures.

At an industry level, a significant amount of activity is planned across all sectors surveyed. Plans in the financial sector are ubiquitous, with 43% of this group indicating they intend to implement extranet technologies, 31% intranets and digital signatures, and 26% interactive voice response. Education also has significant implementation plans; for instance, 30% of this group intends to implement extranets, 22% intranet, and 24% an electronic kiosk. Health indicates a lot of activity with 44% and 42% planning to implement intranets and extranet technologies, respectively. In addition, 33% are planning a company web site and firewalls, and 30% foresee using digital signatures. Most of the businesses surveyed have been engaged in some form of e-commerce to the fore, its potential as a means of buying and selling. The survey paved the way for the development of a complete and comprehensive theoretical framework.

This chapter discussed an initial exploratory survey that examined the extent of e-commerce adoption in Australia and New Zealand. We presented the findings of potential versus achieved benefits and potential versus perceived risks, followed by a comparison of the findings between Europe, Australia, and New Zealand. Finally, we conclude the chapter with two groups of e-commerce adopters, lessons learned, recommendations, and the future of e-commerce in Australia and New Zealand. The next chapter presents a review of the current literature in business to business e-commerce and trust.

Chapter III

Literature Review

In chapter 2, we discussed the findings of an initial exploratory survey. In this chapter we undertake an in-depth literature review of business-to-business e-commerce and the importance of trust.

The task of undertaking a literature review is challenging, especially when it involves theories from multiple disciplines. The chapter begins with a discussion of e-commerce from two perspectives: a technological perspective (including technology trust mechanisms), and a social perspective (discussing trust behaviours in business relationships). Incorporated into the analysis are previous theories that focus on organizational behaviour (inter-organizational relationships), economic perspective (transaction-cost-economics theory), and political perspective (resource dependency theory). The rest of the chapter is organized as follows. First, we discuss the literature pertaining to the need for inter-organizational trust and provide definitions of trust from multi-disciplines, as well as characteristics and the development of trust in business relationships. This is followed by a discussion of the perceived benefits, perceived risks, and technology trust mechanisms in e-commerce leading to outcomes of e-commerce participation. Then, we examine the organizational, economic, and political theories leading to the evolution of inter-organizational systems to inter-organizational trust. Finally, we conclude the chapter with the development of the conceptual model of inter-organizational trust in e-commerce participation, leading to a justification of the research propositions derived from the model.

THE NEED FOR INTER-ORGANIZATIONAL TRUST

In spite of the efficiency and coordination benefits documented in both research literature and the trade press, e-commerce growth was relatively slow when this study was initiated in 1997. The findings of the KPMG e-commerce survey (1999 – discussed in chapter 2) indicated that Internet e-commerce growth was slower within the Asia-Pacific region as compared to the United States. This was due to perceived risks in security of business-to-business transactions and a lack of trust among trading partners (Drummond, 1995; Hudoklin and Stadler, 1997; Keen, 1999; Nath et al., 1998; Storreston, 1998). Fears about electronic fraud and lack of privacy hampered Internet commerce (Gorriz, 1999).

Trust has been identified as one of the central constructs in relationship marketing theory (Morgan and Hunt, 1994). The past decade has seen a paradigm shift toward relational marketing, which encompasses relational contracting, working partnerships, and strategic alliances (Anderson and Narus, 1990; Dwyer, Schurr and Oh, 1987; MacNeil, 1980; Morgan and Hunt, 1994). Relational marketing includes activities directed toward establishing, developing, and maintaining successful relational exchanges. Relational exchanges include supplier partnerships (goods suppliers, just-in-time, and total quality management), lateral partnerships (competitors, technology alliances, nonprofit organizations, government), buyer partnerships (ultimate customers and intermediate customers), and internal partnerships (functional departments, employees, and business units).

Previous research on trust in marketing and management suggests a focus on transaction-specific investments and firms' performance (Doney and Cannon, 1997; Ganesan, 1994; Smith and Barclay, 1997; Zaheer et al., 1998). For example, trust in buyer-seller relations may be an important source of competitive advantage because it lowers transaction costs, increases satisfaction (Geyskens et al., 1998), and facilitates investments, along with other favorable outcomes (Barney and Hansen, 1994; Dyer and Chu, 2000; Gulati, 1995;

Keen, 2000; Pavlou and Ba, 2000; Williamson, 1985). Research has also proposed that competitive advantage is too narrow a determinant for e-commerce adoption. Contemporary research on trust is converging towards a definition reflecting vulnerability, uncertainty, and risks (Das and Teng, 1998; Gambetta, 1998; Mayer et al., 1995; Parkhe, 1998; Sitkin and Pablo, 1992). Trust may also operate as a governance mechanism (Bradach and Eccles, 1989; McKnight and Chervany, 2001) that diminishes opportunistic behaviors in exchange relations and promotes cooperation. Thus, buyer-seller interactions can be modeled along two dimensions; first, integrative interactions characterized by cooperative behaviors that satisfy the objectives of both trading partners; and second, distributive interactions characterized by competitive behaviors directed towards self-interest at the expense of the other trading partners (Mohr and Spekman, 1994).

Granovetter (1985) argues that social relations rather than institutional arrangements lead to trust. As the duration and intensity of interactions between trading partners increase, bonds will develop. This line of reasoning is consistent with Fukuyama (1995), who claims that national efficiencies are highly correlated with an existence of high trust in institutional environments. He argues that *"the economic success of a nation as well as its ability to compete is conditioned by the level of trust inherent in the society"* (Fukuyama, 1995, p.7).

Effective competition in the global economy demands trustworthy trading partners. While it is important for a supplier to gain the trust of a distributor, it is equally imperative that distributors (buyers) trust the supplier (Ganesan, 1994; Kozak and Cohen, 1997). Trust is required to achieve cooperation and commitment because the existence of trust encourages trading partners to:

- work at preserving relationship investments by cooperating with exchange partners;

- resist attractive short-term alternatives in favour of expected long-term benefits of staying with existing trading partner relationships; and

- view potentially high-risk actions as carefully as possible, as commitment and trust exists in trading partners. Trust produces outcomes that promote efficiency, productivity, and effectiveness (Ganesan, 1994; Morgan and Hunt, 1994). In short, commitment and trust lead directly to cooperative behaviours for relationship marketing success.

Similarly, Hart and Saunders (1997) conducted a study on power and trust in EDI adoption. They discovered that trust played a very important role in EDI adoption for two main reasons:

(1) Trust encourages organizations to make investments necessary for electronic information exchange, including the technical investments needed for supporting greater information exchange across organizational boundaries. This, in turn, contributes to improved inter-organizational coordination and information sharing in e-commerce integration. It is important to reinforce trust during the e-commerce implementation process, as trading partners are encouraged and motivated to make investments in computer integration. Over time there will be an increase in e-commerce performance and information sharing; and

(2) Trust discourages opportunistic behaviours that would clearly reduce information sharing over time. Here, trust helps reduce a firm's probability of behaving in an opportunistic way, thus mitigating risks and reinforcing the opportunity to expand information sharing over time.

TRADING PARTNER TRUST

Trust is a concept that has received attention in many social science fields including psychology, sociology, political sciences, economics, marketing, anthropology, and history (see Anderson and Narus, 1990; Cummings and Bromiley, 1996; Dwyer, Schurr, and Oh, 1987; Gambetta, 1988; Ganesan, 1994; Lewicki and Bunker, 1996; Moorman, Deshpande, and Zaltman, 1993; Williamson, 1991). Recently, the role of trust in business has drawn increased attention from management researchers and practitioners alike (Hosmer, 1995; Mayer et al., 1995; Kramer and Tyler, 1996).

Trust in inter-organizational settings can be developed through:

•   Institutionalized processes or routines that enable trading partners to deal fairly and reliably (McKnight et al., 1998; Zaheer et al., 1998; Zucker, 1986);

•   Alignment with economic incentives through hostages, or economic incentive-based trust (Williamson, 1985);

- Social relationships and embedded ties leading to relationship-based trust (Dow et al., 1998; Granovetter, 1985; Gulati, 1995).

Arunachalam (1997) conducted a study analysing issues in EDI adoption and suggested that establishing mutually beneficial trading relationships and customer service appears to be an important consideration for EDI adoption. Handy (1995) suggests that the more virtual organizations are, the more their people need to rely on trust. Virtuality requires trust to make it work; technology alone is not enough (Handy, 1995). It is not an exaggeration to say that trust more than technology drives the growth of e-commerce in all its forms (Keen, 2000). This is because e-commerce is a shared technology and trust helps ensure that technology is used in ways that are beneficial to both trading partners. Internet commerce has led to intensified global competition, faster technological change, rising costs, and risks in developing new products (Parkhe, 1998; Reekers and Smithson, 1996).

The marketing and management literature suggests the need for trust in distribution channels (Anderson and Narus, 1990; Morgan and Hunt, 1994), where vulnerabilities created by a high degree of interdependencies is usually found in channel relationships (Kumar, Scheer, and Steenkamp, 1995). In a typical distribution channel arrangement (between manufacturer-distributor or manufacturer-supplier), switching costs can be relatively high (Doney and Canon, 1997). Trust can also be viewed as a dyadic interpersonal phenomenon because both trading partners are dependent on each other (Ring and Van de Ven, 1992).

Sako (1992:48) stated *"trust between buyer-supplier organizations is critical to the exchange of open and truthful information, especially when proprietary information such as, sales, orders, and inventories or information on future business plans facilitate collaboration."*

Although the importance of trust has been acknowledged, how it develops and functions has received little theoretical attention (McAllister, 1995; Sako, 1998). It was found that trust is not automatically reciprocal (Cummings and Bromiley, 1996). For example, if A trusts B, it does not follow that B necessarily trusts A. The mere fact that A knows and accepts B's future actions does not make the opposite true. While trust is not reciprocal, it is not objective either (Cummings and Bromiley, 1996). Trust is the result of the subjective evaluations and personal perceptions one trading partner makes on another (Gambetta, 1988). Hence, individual trust can also mean inter-organizational trust because trust is derived from individuals in an organization, and is essentially a cumulative process (Hicks, 1999). The next section discusses characteristics and behaviors of trust in business relationships.

Trading Partner Trust Characteristics

Despite the importance of trust, scholarly inquiry into the topic has been hampered, as little academic research has attempted to empirically document the factors affecting trust in marketing relationships (Anderson and Weitz, 1989; Dwyer and Oh, 1987; Dyer and Chu, 2000). Numerous researchers have proposed that trust is essential for interpersonal and group behavior, managerial effectiveness, economic exchanges, and social or political stability. Yet, according to a majority of these researchers, this concept has never been precisely defined. A lack of clarity in the definition of trust has led to an overall picture of confusion, ambiguity, conflicting interpretations, and absence of reliable principles (Hosmer, 1995). In fact, no study has attempted to develop a complete and comprehensive theoretical framework of factors that influence trading partner trust in business-to-business e-commerce participation. Tables 1 through 5 outline the definitions of trust from previous research and multi-disciplines, namely; marketing, management, sociology, psychology, and information systems, that assisted in identifying and developing the definition and types of trading partner trust applied in this study.

Table 1: Definitions of trust from previous research in the marketing discipline

Authors Source	Discipline	Definition of Trust
Anderson and Narus (1990)	*Marketing*	A firm's belief that another company will perform actions that will result in positive outcomes for the firm, as well as not taking unexpected actions that would result in negative outcomes for the firm.
Ganesan (1994)	*Marketing*	Willingness to rely on an exchange partner in confidence.
Kumar (1996)	*Marketing*	Trust is stronger than fear. Partners that trust each other generate greater profits, serve customers better, and are more adaptable.
Moorman, Deshpande and Zaltman (1993)	*Marketing*	Willingness to rely on an exchange partner with whom one has confidence. Also, trust has been viewed as (1) a belief, sentiment, or expectation; and as (2) a behavioural intention that reflects reliance on trading partners and involves vulnerability and uncertainty on the part of the trustor.
Schurr and Ozane (1987, p 940)	*Marketing*	The belief that a party's word or promise is reliable and a party will fulfil its obligations in an exchange relationship.

Table 2: Definitions of trust from previous research in the management discipline

Authors Source	Discipline	Definition of Trust
Barney and Hansen (1994)	Management	Mutual confidence that no party in an exchange will exploit one another's vulnerabilities.
Bromiley and Cummings (1992)	Management	Expectation that another individual or group will (1) have good faith and make efforts to behave in accordance with any commitments, both explicit or implicit, (2) be honest in whatever negotiations precede those commitments, and (3) not take excessive advantage of others even when the opportunity (to renegotiate) is available.
Dyer and Chu (2000)	Management	One party's confidence that the other party in the exchange relationship will not exploit its vulnerabilities.
Gabarro (1987)	Management	Consistency of behaviour such that judgement about trust in working relationships is based on the accumulation of interactions, specific incidents, problems, and events.
Hosmer (1995)	Management	Expectation by one person, group, or firm upon voluntarily accepted duty on the part of another person, group, or firm to recognize and protect the rights and interests of all others engaged in a joint endeavour or economic exchange.
Mayer, Davis and Schoorman (1995)	Management	Willingness of a party to be vulnerable to the actions of another party based on the expectation that the other will perform a particular action important to the trustor, irrespective of the ability to monitor or control that other party.
McAllister (1995)	Management	Cognition based on the concept that we choose whom we will trust, in what respects, and under what circumstances; affective foundations of trust consist of emotional bonds between trading partners.
Mishra (1996)	Management	A party's willingness to be vulnerable to another party based on the belief that the latter party is a) competent, b) open, c) concerned, and d) reliable (Mishra, 1996).
Morgan and Hunt (1994)	Management	Trust exists when one party has confidence in an exchange partner's reliability and integrity.
O'Brien (1995)	Management	An expectation about the positive actions of other people, without being able to influence or monitor the outcome.
Ring and Van de Ven (1994)	Management	Trust as confidence implies: a) the behaviour of another will conform to one's expectation, and b) the goodwill of another.

Table 3: Definitions of trust from previous research in the sociology discipline

Authors Source	Discipline	Definition of Trust
Deutsch (1958)	Sociology	Actions that increase one's vulnerability to the other.
Fukuyama (1995)	Sociology	Exceptions that arise within a community of regular, honest, and cooperative parties, based on commonly shared norms, on the part of other members of that community.
Gambetta (1988, p. 217)	Sociology	Probability that one economic actor will make decisions and take actions that will be beneficial or at least not detrimental to another.
Lewicki and Bunker (1996)	Sociology	A state involving confident, positive expectation about another's motives with respect to oneself in situations entailing risk.
Lewis and Weigert (1986)	Sociology	Undertaking of a risky course of action on the confident expectation that all persons involved in the action will act competently and dutifully.
Sako (1998)	Sociology	An expectation held by an agent that its trading partner will behave in a mutually acceptable manner (including an expectation that neither party will exploit the other's vulnerabilities).
Zucker (1986, p. 50)	Sociology	A set of logical expectations shared by everyone involved in an economic exchange.

Table 4: Definitions of trust from previous research in the psychology discipline

Authors Source	Discipline	Definition of Trust
Doney and Cannon (1997)	Psychology	Perceived credibility and benevolence of a target of trust.
Sabel (1993, p. 1133)	Psychology	The mutual confidence that no party to an exchange will exploit the other's vulnerability. Trust is today widely regarded as a precondition for competitive success.

Table 5: Definitions of trust from previous research in the information systems discipline

Authors Source	Discipline	Definition of Trust
Keen (1999)	Information Systems	Confidence in the business relationship. The definition is extended to include risk, and it focuses on the relationships that directly involve computers and telecommunications, thus creating a trust bond (security, safety, honesty, consumer-protection laws, contracts, privacy, reputation, brand, mutual self-interest).
Ratnasingam and Pavlou (2002; 2003)	Information Systems	The subjective probability with which organizational members collectively assess that a particular transaction will occur according to their confident expectations

Characteristics in the Definition of Trust

Based on the definitions of trust presented in Tables 1-5, the following characteristics of trust were derived:

- A rational (or objective) view which is based on an economic perspective emphasizing the confidence in the predictability of one's expectations. There is a focus on the credible and confident expectations that arise in relation to a trading partner's expertise, skills, reliability, and intentions (Anderson and Weitz, 1989; Barney and Hansen, 1994; Dwyer and Oh, 1987; Ganesan, 1994; Morgan and Hunt, 1994; Moorman et al., 1992; Ring and Van de Ven, 1992). In e-commerce, this view refers to organizational credibility (i.e., the extent to which a buyer believes that the supplier has the required expertise) and competence to perform the job effectively and reliably (Doney and Cannon, 1997).

- A relational (or subjective) view which is based on a social perspective emphasizing confidence in another trading partner's goodwill. Goodwill between trading partners focuses on faith and moral integrity and includes (Lewicki and Bunker, 1996; Mayer et al., 1995; McKnight et al., 1998; Jones and George, 1998). Researchers have also claimed that trust is a behaviour reflecting reliance which involves risks, uncertainties, and vulnerabilities on the part of the trustor (Coleman, 1990; Das and Teng, 1996; Lewis and Weigert, 1986; Parkhe, 1998). Parkhe (1998) identified trust with an element of risk, uncertainty, and vulnerability. Parkhe (1998) was consistent with other researchers who claimed that trust involves risk taking (Chiles and Mackmin, 1996; Das and Teng, 1998; Coleman, 1990; Deutsch, 1958; Koller, 1978; Lewis and Weigert, 1986; Sitkin and Pablo, 1992).

Trust-Building Mechanisms in Business Relationships

This section examines characteristics of trust behaviours from previous research that help to build trust in business relationships, leading to an identification of three types of trust applied in this study.

Dwyer, Schurr, and Oh (1987)

Dwyer, Schurr, and Oh (1987) suggest five phases in the development of trading partner relationships:

(1) Awareness occurs when trading partner A initially recognizes that trading partner B is a feasible exchange partner. In e-commerce, screening of trading partners is usually conducted to determine the most suitable trading partner.

(2) Exploration is seen when a trading partner searches and tries purchases. The benefits and risks of trading relationships are considered. The exploration phase in turn is comprised of five sub-processes: attraction, communication and bargaining, development and exercise of power, norm development, and expectation development.

(3) Expansion occurs when trading partners continually aim to increase their benefits, thus leading to trading partner satisfaction in each other's performance. For example, when a trading partner fulfils the perceived exchange, and obligations are met in an exemplary fashion, the other trading partner's attraction is increased.

(4) Commitment is an implicit or explicit pledge of relational continuity between trading partners. In bilateral relationships, commitment is based on governance structures and/or shared values. Commitment connotes solidarity and cohesion as characterized by durability and consistency.

(5) Durability in the exchange over time. According to MacNeil, (1980, p. 95) *"organic solidarity consists of a common belief in effectiveness of future exchange."* Durability presumes that trading partners can discern the benefits attributable to the exchange relation and anticipate an environment that will continue to be an effective exchange. The Dwyer et al. (1987) study contributed to an understanding of trading partner relationship and trust development.

Gabarro (1987)

Gabarro (1987) suggests that working relationships and social relationships develop over time and can vary in stability, mutuality, and efficiency. He conducted a study of newly appointed company presidents and examined their processes in developing working relationships with key subordinates. His findings suggest that trust in open communications is seen as clear, consistent communication, and when trading partners keep their word. The process is seen as an "interpersonal contract" governed by a set of mutual expectations concerning performance, roles, trust, and influence. In addition, Gabarro (1987) identified four stages of development in new working relationships. They included:

Stage 1 - orientation process, where employees form an impression about one another,

Stage 2 - exploration process, lasting a few months, where tentative expectations become more specific and concrete,

Stage 3 - tests the trust in their relationships. It could take between six months to a year to do this. The interpersonal contract limits each other's influence and gets into shape, and

Stage 4 - emphasizes stabilizing the interpersonal contract as it becomes defined and expectations undergo little changes.

He suggested that trust can be characterized in different ways, including predictability, communication openness, and creditability (the degree to which one person feels assured that another will not take malevolent or arbitrary actions). The Gabarro (1987) study examined the development of working relationships with key subordinates thus contributing to inter-organizational trust.

Doney and Cannon (1997)

Doney and Cannon (1997) examined a study of buyer-supplier relationships. Their findings indicated that the development of trust involved five processes, namely:

(1) A calculative process where trading partners calculate the costs and/or rewards of interacting with another trading partner. Most organizations, when implementing e-commerce, undertake a cost-benefit analysis.

(2) A capability process, which involves determining another trading partner's ability to meet one's obligations, thereby focusing primarily on the credibility component of trust.

(3) A predictive process, which relies on one trading partner's ability to forecast another trading partner's behaviour based on repeated interactions, thereby enabling trading partners to interpret outcomes. For example, through repeatedly making promises and delivering on them, a salesperson develops the confidence of buying firms. Extending this line of reasoning, Lewicki and Bunker (1996) describe predictability as a source of trust that requires not only repeated (consistent) interactions, but also courtship (Shapiro et al., 1992).

(4) An intentionality process, which occurs when the trustor interprets words and behaviours, and attempts to determine intentions in an exchange.

Trust emerges through interpretation and assessment of the other trading partner's motives.

(5)   A transference process, which involves a pattern of gaining trust through reputation and recommendation. This process uses a third party's definition of another as a basis for defining the other as trustworthy. The Doney and Cannon (1997) study contributed to processes involved in trust development in buyer-supplier relationships.

Ring and Van de Ven (1994)

Ring and Van de Ven (1994) developed a framework describing how inter-organizational relationships emerge, evolve, and dissolve. They suggest that cooperative inter-organizational relationships consist of repetitive sequences of negotiations, commitment, and execution stages. During the negotiation stage, trading parties develop joint (not individual) expectations about their motivations, possible investments, and perceived uncertainties as they explore business deals. Repeated efforts in negotiations through formal bargaining and informal sense-making processes provide trading partners with opportunities to assess uncertainties associated with the deal. The commitment stage aims to fulfil trading partners' desires. They reach an agreement on obligations and rules for future action in the relationship. The governance structure of the relationship is established at the commitment stage, leading to a formal relational contract or an informal understanding as a psychological contract between trading parties. In the execution stage, they carry out rules of action and commitment. Trading parties give orders to their subordinates, buy materials, pay the amounts agreed upon, and administer whatever is necessary to execute the agreement. The Ring and Van de Ven (1994) study emphasized the evolvement of inter-organizational relationships that was found relevant for this study as we examined the evolvement of inter-organizational trust in e-commerce participation

Mayer, Davis, and Schoorman (1995)

Mayer, Davis, and Schoorman (1995) identified three trust behaviours that can help establish trustworthiness. They include:

(1)   Skills, competence, and characteristics of trading parties that enable one trading partner to have some influence on another trading partner;

(2) Benevolence or wanting to do good to the trustor, aside from an egocentric profit motive. Benevolence suggests the trustee has some specific attachment to the trustor; and

(3) Integrity in the trustor's perception that occurs when the trustee adheres to a set of principles making them reliable and predictable (if they behave consistently).

The Mayer et al. (1995) study contributed to the definition and an initial awareness that different behavioural characteristics exist in different stages of trading partner trust development.

Mishra (1996)

Mishra (1996) defines trust as one trading partner's willingness to be vulnerable to another trading partner, based on the belief that the latter party is competent, open, caring, and reliable. These dimensions help reinforce trust and build interest in sustaining the other organization as a trading partner over time. The dimensions include:

(1) Competence, which identifies a trading partner's ability to interpret information correctly, thereby enabling correct and accurate decisions. Consistent, competent behaviour contributes to a trading partner's credibility. The greater the credibility, the greater the confidence and willingness to trust the other trading partner and value the relationship.

(2) Openness is the ability of one trading partner to affect changes in another trading partner (being flexible to changes) based on honesty. Openness implies that a trading partner is willing to listen to new ideas and share information, rather than control a situation or withhold information (a situation of imbalance of power), thus reinforcing trust. Such demonstrations in turn reduce the probability that the other trading partner will behave opportunistically. Openness to change improves efficiencies which reinforces mutual interest in preserving the continuity of the relationship. Continuity in turn reinforces confidence that a trading partner will not behave opportunistically, (i.e., such as inappropriately using information, misleading, cheating, or lying).

(3) Caring indicates that one trading partner will act in ways designed to benefit the other trading partner. Caring leads to concern that trading partners believe they will not be taken advantage of.

(4) Reliability is seen in consistency between what a trading partner says and what they actually do. Reliability determines the extent to which trading partners can depend on each other and checks whether trading partners can follow through on promises. Reliability reinforces cooperation which in turn reinforces trust. Cooperation is the complementary, coordinated action taken by organizations and interdependent relationships to achieve mutual outcomes with expected reciprocation over time. Therefore, trust at an inter-organizational level is important. The Mishra (1996) study contributed to different trust behaviours in a trading partner relationship.

Lewicki and Bunker (1996)

Lewicki and Bunker (1996) extended the work of Shapiro et al. (1992) by taking a psychological perspective. They argued that the development of trust occurs in stages, with deterrence-based being the first and identification-based the last stage, or the highest level of trust. They also suggested that the development of trust is the same for all types of relationships, be they romantic, manager-employee, among peers, or among trading partners in e-commerce. Figure 5 portrays a three-stage model of trust development. Based upon the work of Shapiro, Sheppard, and Cheraskin (1992), this model identifies three

Figure 5: Three stages in the development of trust

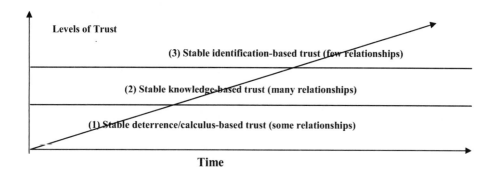

types of trust: deterrence-based trust, knowledge-based trust, and identification-based trust.

(1) Deterrence-based trust emphasizes the behavioural consistency of trading partners (as in trading partners' willingness to do what they say they are going to do). Although the threat of punishment in deterrence-based trust was seen as a negative factor, economic gains and rewards were seen as calculative measures. Lewicki and Bunker (1996) suggest that deterrence-based trust is grounded not only in the fear of punishment for violating trust, but also in the rewards derived from fulfilling actions (also known as calculus-based trust). This is particularly true in the case of the automotive industry. Ford applied power when the EDI network was introduced. Ford made it clear to its established suppliers that they should use EDI. Ford did provide suppliers with initial training and its software to run on IBM machines. Suppliers with incompatible systems or with no systems at all were requested to find appropriate solutions as quickly as possible. Clearly, this was a situation where coercive power exercised by Ford was seen in establishing connections that involved the expense of the suppliers in buying new equipment. Dependence can arise due to limited supply alternatives or from an imbalance of power between suppliers and car manufacturers. Furthermore, the inconvenience of having to use Ford's system in addition to other systems for trading with other customers was another issue, especially at a time when the smaller suppliers were unaware of EDI's potential.

(2) Knowledge-based trust is grounded in behavioural predictability based on prior knowledge and past experiences with the other trading partner (that is, the trustee). One trading partner can predict the behaviour of another trading partner.

(3) Identification-based trust is based on empathy, concern, and common values for another trading partner's desires and intentions to the extent that one trading partner is able to act as an agent for the other. Identification-based trust tends to revolve around a common task rather than being based on individual cues.

The trust model by Lewicki and Bunker (1996) suggest that deterrence-based trust depend on the willingness to believe that there is a credible threat of punishment for a failure to cooperate. Knowledge-based trust assumes that people's dispositions are well known, and their behaviour can be reliably predicted. This model is consistent with rational choice motivations. Finally, identification-based trust occurs when one trading partner fulfils the needs and desires of the other trading partner and acts in ways to realize joint gains. The Lewicki and Bunker (1996) study contributed to the stability of trading partner relationships and confirmed that trust develops gradually from one stage to another.

McAllister (1995)

McAllister (1995) focused on two principal forms of interpersonal trust. First, cognition-based trust (or rational trust) grounded in an individual's belief about peer reliability and dependability, and second, affect-based trust (or emotional trust) grounded in reciprocated interpersonal care and concerns or feelings of closeness and goodwill. Positive aspects of cognitive-based trust were seen in reliability, competence, fairness, and consistency of both trading partners. Over time these evolved into affective or emotional trust. Affective-based trust includes faith, care, concern, openness, encouragement, and information-sharing between trading partners. Cognitive and affective founda-tions of trust suggest that we choose whom we will trust, in what respects, and under which circumstances. We base the choice on what we take to be good reasons, constituting evidence of trustworthiness (Lewis and Weigert, 1985). In working relationships that involve high interdependencies, peer performance can have a determining impact on personal productivity. The McAllister (1995) study contributed to different trust behaviours derived from two dimensions (i.e., a cognitive-rational versus an affective-emotional perspective).

Barney and Hansen (1994)

Barney and Hansen (1994) identified three types of trust:

(1) Weak trust, characterized by trading partners who have mutual confi-dence that others will not exploit their vulnerabilities. They do not depend on contractual or other forms of governance mechanisms. The weak form of trust emerges in the case of limited opportunities for opportunism (Das and Teng, 1996; Parkhe, 1998; Sitkin and Pablo, 1992).

(2) Semi-strong trust depends on governance mechanisms such as reputation and contracts to safeguard against opportunism. Semi-strong trust occurs

when significant exchange vulnerabilities exist and trust emerges from the
protection of contracts. High costs are imposed on trading partners who
behave opportunistically. Semi-strong trust can be an advantage, particularly when competitors use different governance methods, skills, and
abilities that are costly to initiate.

(3)   Strong trust (or principled trust) emerges as a response to set, internalized
norms and principles guiding trading partners' behaviour. It is independent of whether or not specific governance mechanisms exist, and is
difficult to imitate. Previous scholars propose that trust exists in exchange
relationships because of risks from the constant threat of opportunistic
behaviours that is linked with governance (Hill, 1990; Williamson, 1975).
The Barney and Hansen (1994) study contributed to different types of
trust behaviours and their relation to governance mechanisms.

Sako (1998)
Sako (1998) identified three types of trust:

(1)   Contractual trust hinges on the other trading partner's ability to abide by
contractual agreements. Contractual trust rests on shared norms of
honesty, promise keeping, a shared understanding of professional conduct, and technical and managerial standards.

(2)   Competence trust relies on the other trading partner's likelihood of
following through with her or his promises. It is the ability of trading
partners to adhere to the business operations.

(3)   Goodwill trust relies on trading partners' commitment, and mutual benefits. Goodwill trust can only exist if there is consensus on the principle of
fairness. Goodwill trust includes collaboration and is seen as highly
cooperative (attempting to satisfy another trading partner's needs), and
highly assertive (attempting to satisfy one's own needs). Sako's (1998)
study contributed to three types of trust behaviours, suggesting that trust
develops in stages.

Zucker (1986)
Zucker (1986) identified three sources of trust:

(1)   Process-based trust is derived from concrete experiences of social and/ or economic exchanges. It assumes an expectation for future transactions deeply rooted in stable personal relations. This view is consistent with Granovetter (1985) and Fukuyama (1995), who suggest that there is social embeddedness in economic actions.

(2)   Characteristic-based trust relies on personal characteristics such as age, sex, and belonging to a particular ethnic community or social system. Exchanges are limited to those with a common cultivated system, shared background, and expectations.

(3)   Institutional-based trust transcends concrete exchange experiences, and does not depend upon the exchange partner. Sources of institutional-based trust include all traditions, professions, certifications, licenses, and brand names. Zucker's (1986) study contributed to the sources of trust in this study.

Morgan and Hunt (1994)

Morgan and Hunt (1994) proposed a model for relationship marketing. It is called the "Key Mediating Variables" (KMV) model, which focuses on trading partner relationships. They proposed that relationship commitment and trust are mediating variables for five antecedents of trust, namely: relationship termination costs, relationship benefits, shared values, communication, and opportunistic behaviour. The model also has five outcomes, namely: acquiescence, propensity to leave, cooperation, functional conflict, and decision-making uncertainty. The model suggests that trading partners do not trust commercial web providers from a lack of shared values, which could lead to lower relationship commitment. This in turn could generate higher decision-making uncertainties, less cooperation, and a higher propensity to leave. The Morgan and Hunt (1994) study identified trust behaviours that contributed to relationship commitment in this study.

Dyer and Chu (2000)

Dyer and Chu (2000) suggest that trust consists of three components, namely: reliability, fairness, and goodwill. Trust is based on the confidence expected to emerge in situations where the trustworthy trading partner in the exchange relationship:

(1)   Is known to reliably make good faith efforts to behave in accordance with prior commitments;

(2)   Makes adjustments (as market conditions change) in ways perceived as fair by the exchange partner; and

(3)   Does not take excessive advantage of an exchange partner even when the opportunity is available. The Dyer and Chu (2000) study contributed to trust behaviours in a trading partner exchange relationship.

An analysis of trust behaviours and characteristics in business relationships examined in the previous section indicated that trust takes time to develop and that there are distinct characteristics in each stage of trust. Table 6 summarizes the trust characteristics and behaviours from previous research and contributes to the identification of three types of trust discussed in the next section.

Types of Trading Partner Trust

We identify three types of trust from a synthesis of the above discussion of trust. They include competence trust, predictability trust, and goodwill trust that gradually develop from one stage to another.

Competence Trading Partner Trust

Previous research at an organizational and inter-organizational level suggests that the competency dimension of trust is discussed in the context of exchange relationships (Sako, 1992). The extent to which one supplier organization's products meet the quality needs of the buying organization, and the buying organization no longer inspects those products before accepting delivery, shows greater trust in the supplier organization's competence (Sako, 1992; Dyer and Chu, 2000). This view was consistent with the findings of the exploratory study when Ford stopped checking the goods delivered by their suppliers.

The first stage competence trust emphasizes trust in a trading partner's skill, technical knowledge, and ability to operate business-to-business e-commerce applications correctly and to do what they are supposed to do (Gabarro, 1987; Lewicki and Bunker, 1996; Mayer et al., 1995; Mishra, 1996). In addition, it also examines the compatibility of e-commerce systems and technology trust mechanisms. Competence trust involves a formal (objective) calculative process of business transactions. It focuses on economic benefits derived from the trading partner's ability and skills to correctly operate e-commerce technologies. Trading partners apply performance assessments as a checking mechanism to evaluate competence trust.

Trading partners who demonstrate competence and have the right skills and expertise in operating e-commerce systems tend to deliver high-quality goods, services, or information to other trading partners (Helper, 1991; Webster, 1995). Thus, competence trust relies on an economic foundation where benefits are derived from savings in costs and time. Alternatively, a lack of competence trust may lead to additional costs if trading partners need to be re-trained, or if the same transaction needs to be re-sent correctly.

Predictability Trading Partner Trust

Predictability trading partner trust is derived from the consistent behaviour of trading partners in the second stage. Consistency between what a trading partner says and actually does makes the partner reliable (Hart and Saunders, 1997). It implies that trading partners are dependable and can follow through on promises; that in turn develops high levels of cooperation and reinforces trust (Dyer and Chu, 2000; Mayer et al., 1995; Mishra, 1996; Zucker, 1986). Predictability trust is an extension of competence-based trust (i.e., a series of positive, consistent, and reliable behaviours) that makes a trading partner predictable and therefore trustworthy (Lewicki and Bunker, 1996). In addition, consistent behaviours of trading partners lead to a foundation of familiarity and are based on the prior history of trading experiences and a trading partner's tolerance for mistakes. Alternatively, a series of negative consistent behaviours (i.e., a lack of competence trust, opportunistic behaviours, and an imbalance of power among trading partners) can lead to predictability mistrust.

Goodwill Trading Partner Trust

Goodwill trading partner trust occurs when a trading partner believes the other trading partner is honest and dependable (Barney and Hansen, 1994; Dyer and Chu, 2000; Mayer et al., 1995; McAllister, 1995; Mishra, 1996; Sako, 1998). Goodwill trust develops from both competence and predictability trust. When expectations of reliability and dependability are met, trust moves to affective foundations that include emotional bonds such as care and concern. It emphasizes a belief in a trading partner's care, concern, honesty, and benevolence that permits other trading partners to further invest in their trading partner relationships. This, in turn, leads to a foundation of empathy characterized by an increased level of cooperation, open communication, information sharing, and commitment to increased participation in e-commerce, thus leading to three stages of trust development. Trading partners who demonstrate care and concern are willing to share information and commit to long-term investments. Goodwill trust occurs when the primary reliance is on moral character. The next section discusses the benefits of the three types of trading partner trust. While Table 6 presents the three types of trust characteristics, Table 7 presents the sub-concepts and definitions of trading partner trust.

Table 6: Types of trust in business relationships

Types of Trust Sources	1st Stage Competence Trading Partner Trust Economic Foundation	2nd Stage Predictability Trading Partner Trust Familiarity Foundation	3rd Stage Goodwill Trading Partner Trust Empathic Foundation
Zucker (1986)	Process-based trust	Characteristics-based trust	Institutional-based trust
Gabarro (1987)	Character Role competence	Judgment	Motives/ Intentions
Sako (1992)	Contractual	Competence	Goodwill
Barney and Hansen(1994)	Weak form of trust	Semi-strong form of trust	Strong form of trust
Mayer, Davis and Schoorman (1995)	Ability	Integrity	Benevolence
McAllister (1995)	Cognitive	Cognitive → affective	Affective
Lewicki and Bunker (1996)	Deterrence/ Calculus	Knowledge	Identification
Mishra (1996)	Competence	Reliability	Openness Care Concern
Dyer and Chu (2000)	Reliability	Fairness	Goodwill

Table 7: Sub-concepts and definitions of trust in trading partners

Construct	Sub-Concepts	Definition
Trust in Trading Partners		Trust behaviours that determine competence, predictability, and goodwill types of trading partner trust:
	Competence Trust	Reliance upon the ability, skills, knowledge, and competence of a trading partner to perform business-to-business e-commerce correctly and completely. Competence trust examines a trading partner's ability, skills, and level of competence to undertake e-commerce operations and fulfil expectations.
	Predictability Trust	Reliance upon the consistent behaviours of trading partners that allow another trading partner to make predictions and judgments based on prior experiences. Predictability trust examines trading partners' consistent behaviours based on past experiences.
	Goodwill Trust	Reliance upon the care, concern, honesty, and benevolence shown by trading partners that allow the other trading partner to further invest in the trading partner relationship. Goodwill trust examines a trading partner's honesty, care, and concern as well as the willingness to share information, cooperate, and commit to long-term investments.

PERCEIVED BENEFITS OF E-COMMERCE

The survey of literature on the benefits of e-commerce identified three types of benefits. These include perceived economic, relationship-related, and strategic benefits discussed below. Perceived benefits of e-commerce technologies (applications) indicate that organizations' experiences with regards to the benefits have been fairly consistent (Dyer and Chu, 2000; Kalakota and Whinston, 1996; Marcella et al., 1998; Murkohpaday et al., 1995; Nath et al., 1998; Premkumar et al., 1994; Raman, 1996; Sydow, 1998; Vijayasarathy and Robey, 1997; Senn, 2000; Zaheer et al., 1998).

Perceived economic benefits arise from improvements and efficiencies in business processes, as a result of speed and automation of e-commerce applications. These benefits occur because transactions are sent electronically from one application to another. They include a reduction of transaction costs and administrative expenses, time-savings from a faster trading cycle, and improved accuracy because the receiving trading partner need not re-key the data. Perceived economic benefits are derived from operational savings in using e-commerce technologies (Fearson and Philip, 1998; Iacovou et al., 1995; Nath et al., 1998; Senn, 1999).

Murkopdhyay, Kerke, and Kalathur (1995) conducted a study of Chrysler assembly centers and identified that EDI use improved the quality of information exchange and reduced inventory, transportation, and administrative costs. If properly configured, Internet applications can increase and enhance trading partners' productivity, and increase their capability to communicate globally. As more information and services are added to an organization's intranet, business decisions can be made more quickly. Intranets contribute to reduced costs of distributing corporate information such as newsletters and memos. Extranets, on the other hand, offer richer capabilities for information transfers, open new revenue prospects, and decrease costs and cycle times by providing real-time tracking and monitoring information. Small to medium-sized businesses can now leverage Internet systems to reduce paperwork and interface with their trading partners, suppliers, and customers in real-time by taking advantage of "leaner and meaner" extranets (Jevans, 1999; Riggins and Rhee, 1998; Senn, 2000).

Extranet benefits include using familiar Internet tools and interface, increased communication between trading partners that allow for both internal, external communication, and real-time transaction recording. Transactions are duplicated across both the trading partner and supplier databases, thus facilitating a high degree of information sharing and enabling decision makers to make more informed decisions.

Trust in e-commerce networks has a productive value because trust is known to economize transaction and search costs, thereby creating conditions for trading partner exchanges (Carney, 1998; Ganesan, 1994). Economic benefits are derived from sharing initial connection and implementation costs associated in e-commerce. Buyers who trust their suppliers may direct them to purchase hardware and software from particular vendors where discounts are available on those items. In addition, buyers and sellers gain from the compatibility of their systems. Trust not only reduces transaction costs and the cost of monitoring trading partners' performance, but also eliminates the need for installing control systems based on short-term financial results (Cummings and Bromiley, 1996). By sharing e-commerce technologies, trust increases confidence and security in trading partner relationships, thereby promoting open, substantive information exchanges (Gulati, 1995; Handy, 1995; Keen, 1999). Previous research suggests that trust in buyer-supplier relations may be an important source for competitive advantage because it lowers transaction costs (Barney and Hansen, 1994; Dyer and Chu, 2000; Zaheer et al., 1998). In short, trust improves information availability, reduces transaction costs, contributes to positive association, and ameliorates negative externalities.

Perceived relationship-related benefits are derived from positive opportunities that arise from economic benefits. They include increased operational efficiencies, better customer service, improved inter-organizational relationships, and increased ability to compete. The interactive nature of the Web permits access to greater amounts of dynamic information and supports queries for decision-making (Hoffman et al., 1996). For example, intranets provide an economic backbone for enterprise networks through closer contact with customers, suppliers, and employees who are able to access vast amounts of information. Extranets make information more accessible and simple to search, which can accelerate trading partner relationships.

Perceived relationship-related benefits refer to satisfaction that trading partners achieve in their trading partner relationships and from using e-commerce technologies. E-commerce systems such as EDI, intranets, and extranets assist buyer-seller trading partner relationships and improve supplier reliability by improving delivery performance and ensuring an acceptable quality and correct quantity of goods (Walton, 1997). Technical connections derived from e-commerce applications between relationships are often strong, but trading partners in e-commerce organizations play an even more important role in building social bonds. Continued and repeated transactions lead to stronger relationships between trading partners, thereby tying trading partners together economically, technically, and socially. Relationship-related benefits show the presence of effective collaboration and communication between trading partners

Coordination reflects the set of tasks one trading partner expects and the other trading partner performs. Successful trading partner relationships are marked by coordinated actions directed at mutual objectives consistent with organizational interests (Mohr and Spekman, 1994). High levels of communications permit self-disclosure about an organization's needs, priorities, prices, delivery, and terms of agreement and it also enhances an organization's reputation as being fair and equitable (Ozanne and Schurr, 1985).

Mohr and Spekman (1994) identified three aspects of communication that will improve coordination. First, communication quality is defined as accuracy, timeliness, adequacy, correctness, and credibility of information exchanged. Second is the extent of critical and proprietary information shared between trading partners. By sharing information and by being knowledgeable about each other's business, trading partners are able to act independently in maintaining the relationship over time. The systematic availability of information allows people to complete their tasks more effectively and is associated with increased levels of satisfaction, which is an important predictor of a successful trading partner relationship. The third aspect is the extent of participation in planning and goal setting between trading partners. When one trading partner's actions influence the ability of the other to effectively compete, the need for participation in specifying roles, responsibilities, and expectations increases (Mohr and Spekman, 1994). Thus, coordination leads to a smooth flow of communication and satisfaction among trading partners, and leads to stronger commitment.

Commitment is another relational benefit, and is characterized by the willingness of trading partners to exert effort on behalf of their relationship. A high level of commitment contributes to a situation where both trading parties can achieve individual and joint goals without raising their opportunistic behaviours. Thus relationship-related benefits are derived from effective coordination, communication, and commitment.

Communication enables the formal and informal sharing of meaningful and timely information between organizations, which is the key to coordinating trading partners' skills and resources (Anderson and Narus, 1990). Effective communication enables trading partners to benefit from one another, thereby learning the core competencies of its partner. Trading partners who exhibit consistent trust through confidence in the other trading partner's sincerity, reliability, loyalty, and willingness to refrain from opportunistic behaviour are developing predictability trust. Predictability trust develops from consistent positive behaviours and assurances between what the trading partner says and what it actually does that leads to reliability and dependability (Cummings and Bromiley, 1996; Lewicki and Bunker, 1996; Mishra, 1996).

Past studies indicate that organizations with short-term orientation rely on efficiencies from market exchanges to maximize their profits in a transaction, whereas organizations with long-term orientations rely on relational exchanges (repeated exchanges) to maximize their profits over a series of repeated transactions (Doney and Cannon, 1997; Hosmer, 1995; Ganesan, 1994; Morgan and Hunt, 1994). For example, a retailer's trust in a vendor can affect their long-term orientation by reducing the perception of risks associated with opportunistic behaviours. Hazards of opportunistic behaviours in long-term relationships can be mitigated or removed if trust between trading partners exists. Gulati (1995) suggests that trust enables incomplete contracting in dyadic relationships to adapt to unanticipated contingencies in a mutually profitable manner.

Perceived strategic benefits refer to the long-term gains an organization achieves from developing closer ties with its trading partners by using e-commerce to improve its competitive position. Perceived strategic benefits include a compressed business cycle, intensified relationships with trading partners, and the development of corporate strategies (Fearon and Philip, 1998). Yet, perceived strategic benefits are often unseen and difficult to quantify. E-commerce provides decision-making support where strategic use of information becomes available in a computer-usable format. Changes to business processes from the use of e-commerce contribute directly operational improvements (Jamieson, 1996; Kalakota, 1996). For example, e-commerce allows for time-based competitive moves such as quick-response retailing, just-in-time manufacturing, and close-to-zero inventories (Kalakota and Whinston, 1996; Kalakota and Robinson, 2001). In addition, e-commerce helps to achieve the broader goals of improving an organization's image, strengthening its reputation, increasing long-term investments, and reaching new markets (Riggins and Rhee, 1998; Senn, 2000). Others have also suggested that trust is an essential element of e-commerce and can be used as a strategic mechanism for long-term trading partner relationships (Keen, 2000; Speier, 1998).

Similarly, Ganesan (1994) suggests that long-term orientation in buyer-seller relationships is a function of two factors: mutual dependence and the extent to which they trust one another. Anderson and Weitz (1989) suggest that these long-term orientations lead to commitment and a willingness to forego self-interests for mutual benefits. Similarly, Morgan and Hunt (1994) found that the stronger a trading partner's commitment to the relationship, the less likely it is to end the relationship. One reason for continuing a trading partner relationship is satisfaction, as opposed to dependence or bonding by contract. A trading partner who is satisfied with a current relationship is more likely to maintain that relationship than a trading partner who is dissatisfied with the arrangement (Berry, 1999; Cannon and Perrault, 1999; Griffith et al., 2000). For example, Webb and Gile (2001) point out that by concentrating on customers, sellers can build a competitive advantage. Veliyath and Fitzgerland (2000) discuss several ways that customer satisfaction could achieve competitive advantage, among which are identifying, creating, and predicting customer needs.

Commitment is an enduring desire to maintain a valued relationship (Moorman et al., 1992). Morgan and Hunt (1994) suggest that strategic benefits are derived from commitment and trust in marketing relationships that encourage trading partners to: (1) resist attractive short-term alternatives in favor of the future long-term benefits of continuing the relationship; (2) believe in cooperation to preserve and enhance the relationships; and (3) believe that the partner will not act opportunistically. Table 8 below presents the sub-concepts and definitions of perceived benefits of e-commerce.

Table 8: Sub-concepts and definitions of perceived benefits of e-commerce

Construct	Sub-Concepts	Definition
Perceived Benefits of E-Commerce		Perceived benefits of e-commerce are gains received by organizations that have adopted e-commerce.
	Perceived economic benefits of e-commerce	Benefits derived from direct savings in costs and time. Perceived direct benefits examine the speed and savings in costs and time from automation.
	Perceived indirect benefits of e-commerce	Benefits derived from accuracy and quality of e-commerce messages and from competitive advantages lead to trading partner satisfaction. Perceived indirect benefits examine trading partners' sharing of risks, service quality, productivity, and competitive advantage.
	Perceived relationship-related benefits of e-commerce	Benefits derived from closer- trading partner relationships such as open communications, information-sharing cooperation, and commitment. Perceived relationship-related benefits examine communication, information sharing, cooperation and commitment.
	Perceived strategic benefits of e-commerce	Benefits derived from long-term business investments and improved reputation of trading partners. Perceived strategic benefits examine the image, reputation, and long-term investments of a trading partner.

PERCEIVED RISKS OF E-COMMERCE

Perceived risks refer to the weaknesses in e-commerce technologies, trading partner relationships, networks, and e-commerce environment that can increase business risks from the trading partners. Risk has been defined as "the possibility of an adverse outcome, and uncertainty over the occurrence, timing or magnitude of that adverse outcome" (Cavello and Merkhofer, 1994). Perceived risks are negatively associated with transaction intentions (Jarvenpaa et al., 2000), inter-organizational partnerships (Leverick and Cooper, 1998), and joint ventures (Gabrisch, 1993). The fact that the Internet was initially created to primarily share information and not to support business processes implies that no security mechanisms were implicitly included (Chellapa, 2001).

The widespread use of e-commerce has not only changed the way businesses are conducted, but has also introduced new risks that need to be addressed. The Internet, originally designed for scientific research use, has many inherent security flaws. For example, Internet-based EDI security is still an administrative nightmare with problems from eavesdropping, password sniffing, data modification, spoofing, and repudiation (Bhimani, 1996; Drummond, 1994). Other e-commerce risks include snooping, misuse, theft, corruption of information, theft of identity, and personal threats (Stewart, 1998).

Information travelling over the Internet passes through many inter-mediating nodes before reaching the final destination. With millions of transactions in the network, the potential for security breaches becomes even more significant. Trading partners concerned with privacy and security may decide not to undertake commercial transactions over the Internet. Therefore, Internet e-commerce requires effective and trusted mechanisms for ensuring information security and privacy.

E-commerce security risks can occur either internally or externally and can be primarily human or non-human (technology). The risks could be accidental or intentional. Risks can be caused by the disclosure, destruction, and modification of e-commerce transactions, or by denial of service attacks that lead to availability problems and the violation of confidential data. Ring and Van de Ven (1994) suggest various terms to describe risks such as technological, commercial, and corporate risks. Similarly, Das and Teng (1996) used the term "performance risk" to account for the possibility that objectives of inter-organizational relationships are not achieved even though all partners cooperate. Perceived risks of e-commerce in this study are categorized as perceived technology performance-related risks, relational risks, and general risks.

Perceived technology performance-related risks are associated with access to e-commerce infrastructure and involve the hazards of not achieving the performance objectives of a trading partner relationship (Das and Teng, 1996; Lemos, 2001). Trading partners are subject to security attacks and intrusions by hackers. The security break-ins not only result in revenue losses for businesses, but also result in projecting adverse perceptions of e-commerce security (Chellapa and Pavlou, 2001). The information transmitted may be vulnerable at various points including the trading partner's in-house applications, interface, translation software, network connection, or communication management as well as the carrier's network and mailbox services. Cross-vulnerabilities that exist between interdependent trading partners in an e-commerce network can put organizations at risk due to the "domino effect" of one trading partner's security failure compromising the integrity of the other trading partner's system (Jamieson, 1996; Marcella et al., 1998). Trading partners are subject to security attacks and intrusions by hackers. The security break-ins not only result in revenue losses for businesses, but also result in projecting adverse perceptions of e-commerce security (Chellapa and Pavlou, 2001). This is because e-commerce systems do not operate unilaterally, and networks that connect trading partners are often shared. Threats to network security can come from the Internet or from an organization's internal networks. Messages on internal networks may be intercepted due to improper configuration, overly restrictive access controls, or failure to closely monitor the network traffic. It is estimated that eighty to ninety-five percent of the total number of security incidents are due to insider attacks (Brensen, 1996; Chan and David, 2000). Furthermore, it was found that security techniques in existing software and hardware cannot completely assure security (Nath et al., 1998). Hence, internal networks connected to the Internet become exposed to outside intruders, thus contributing to technology performance-related risks.

Perceived relational risks are closely related to risks derived from mistrust (Williamson, 1993). Relational risks develop from a lack of experience and technical knowledge about security, concerns about the auditability of e-commerce, task uncertainties, environment uncertainties, false impressions of unreliability, and concerns about the enforceability of transaction records in the electronic trade area. The automation of e-commerce systems where transactions are processed at high speed and volumes has led to reduced opportunities to spot problems using human intuition (ICAEW, 1992). Thus, timely resolution of errors or problems may be hampered by the potential loss of an audit trail. This could make re-construction and reconciliation of records difficult

(Bhimani, 1996; EDICA, 1990; Jamieson, 1996; Nath et al., 1998). Relational risks such as production delays, disrupted cash flows, legal liability, and loss of profitability can affect anticipated cost savings and business continuity (Jamieson, 1996; Hart and Saunders, 1998; Marcella et al., 1998).

Inter-organizational relationships are often characterized by inherent instability arising from uncertainties of trading partners' future behavior (Parkhe, 1998). Similarly, relational risks are derived when poor cooperative relationships produce the fear that an organization may not work towards the mutual interests of its trading partner or that that it may not cooperate in a manner specified in the trading partner agreement.

Coercive power is often exercised when trading partners lack cooperation. For example, trading partner A is likely to use coercive power when trading partner B does not cooperate. Power can focus on the control of an organization's critical or strategic activities. Implicit in this issue is the concept of organizational inter-dependence (Saunders, 1990). The Hart and Saunders (1997) study of power and trust in EDI adoption suggests that organizations with greater power can influence their trading partners to adopt EDI. Their findings indicate that use of power was negatively related to the volume of EDI transactions. While electronic networks may facilitate easier exchanges, they may not necessarily lead to increases in the frequency of business-to-business transactions. Thus, power exists on two levels: (1) as a motive, and (2) as a behaviour.

Functional conflicts are the result of an imbalance of power, and they can often arise in inter-organizational relationships due to the inherent interdependencies between trading partners. The conflicts between trading partners A and B are influenced by rewards (that are reward sources of power), and deprivations (coercive sources of power). This is particularly true in the case of Ford; when given the incentive to produce in large quantities, manufacturers found that it was necessary to pressure dealers to accept more cars than they desired during slow times. Conflicts tend to decrease the overall level of satisfaction within a relationship (Anderson and Narus, 1990).

Williamson (1975, p 47) suggests that opportunism is *"self-interest seeking with guile."* Opportunism leads to manipulation of information which affects the honesty and integrity of the trading partner (Hill, 1990). In an effort to control self-interested behaviour, trading partners are compelled to negotiate and write explicit legal contracts that generally are time consuming and expensive.

Perceived general risks are primarily derived from poor business practices that include:

- Eavesdropping attacks on a network that can result in the theft of account information such as account balances and billing information;

- Password *sniffing* attacks that can be used to gain access to a system containing proprietary graphic algorithms;

- Data modification attacks that can be used to modify the contents of certain transactions;

- Spoofing, which occurs when unauthorized personnel masquerade as another party. In one such situation, a criminal can set up a storefront and collect thousands or even millions of account numbers or other information from unsuspecting consumers, and;

- Repudiation, which can cause major problems with billing systems and transaction processing agreements.

Table 9 below presents the sub-concepts and definitions of perceived risks of e-commerce. In the next section we discuss technology trust mechanisms in e-commerce.

Table 9: Sub-concepts and definitions of perceived risks of e-commerce

Construct	Sub-Concepts	Definition
Perceived Risks of E-Commerce		Perceived risks of e-commerce are the potential weakness, barriers, and losses faced by organizations that have adopted e-commerce.
	Perceived Technology Performance related risks of e-commerce	Risks derived from misuse of e-commerce technologies, viruses, and the lack of confidentiality, integrity, unauthorized access, or availability mechanisms. Perceived technology performance risks examine the compatibility, infrastructure, complexity, and uncertainties of e-commerce systems and operations.
	Perceived Relational risks of e-commerce	Risks derived from trading partners' lack of knowledge and training in e-commerce. Perceived relationship related risks examine opportunistic behaviour, conflicting attitudes, poor reputation, lack of training, and reluctance to change in trading partners.
	Perceived General risks of e-commerce	Risks derived from poor business practices, environmental risks, lack of standards, and lack of audit policies. Perceived general risks examine existing business practices, policies, and security services.

TECHNOLOGY TRUST MECHANISMS IN E-COMMERCE

Technology trust mechanisms in e-commerce are control safeguards and protection services that provide assurances and guarantees in the form of security. For example, Tan and Thoen (1998) suggest the term "control trust" to refer to embedded protocols, policies, and procedures in e-commerce that help to reduce the risk of opportunistic behaviours among consumers and Web retailers. Similarly, Lee and Turban (2001) measured trustworthiness of Internet shopping based on consumer evaluations of technical competence and Internet performance levels (such as speed, reliability, and availability). Whereas the traditional notion of trust focused on trading partner relationships, trust in e-business also incorporates the notion of technology trust, which is defined as *"the subjective probability by which organizations believe that the underlying technology infrastructure and control mechanisms are capable of facilitating transactions according to their confident expectations"* (Ratnasingam and Pavlou, 2002). Technology trust mechanisms include:

Confidentiality mechanisms that reveal data only to authorized parties who either have a legitimate need to know or have access to the system. Disclosure of transaction content may lead to the loss of confidentiality (privacy) of sensitive information, whether accidentally or deliberately divulged onto an e-commerce network or an EDI mailbox storage system (Caelli et al., 1991; Jamieson, 1996; Marcella et al., 1998). Confidentiality of business-to-business e-commerce transactions is achieved by encrypting the messages.

Integrity mechanisms aim to provide assurance that e-commerce messages and transactions are complete, accurate, and unaltered (Bhimani, 1996; Jamieson, 1996; Parker, 1995; Marcella et al., 1998). Unauthorized access to e-commerce systems can lead to the modification of messages or records of either trading partner, which could lead to fraud.

Errors in the processing and communication of e-commerce systems can result in the transmission of incorrect trading information or inaccurate reporting to management. Application and accounting controls are used to ensure accuracy, completeness, and authorization of inbound transactions from receipt to database update, and outbound transactions from generation to transmission. Accounting controls identify, assemble, analyze, classify, record, and report an organization's transactions that maintain accountability for the related assets and liabilities (EDICA, 1990; Marcella et al., 1998).

Authentication mechanisms establish that trading partners are who they claim they are. Data origin authentication ensures that messages are received from a valid trading partner, and confirms that the trading partner is valid, true, genuine, and worthy of acceptance by reason of conformity. Authentication requires that 1) the sender can be sure that the message reaches the intended recipient, and only the intended recipient; and 2) the recipient can be sure that the message came from the sender and not an imposter. It is important that authentication procedures are included in the organization's security plan, as the lack of these could lead to valuable, sensitive information being revealed to competitors which could affect their business continuity.

Encryption mechanisms provide authentication features that provide security and audit reviews. These reviews ensure e-commerce messages are received only from authorized trading partners (Gentry, 1994; Marcella et al., 1998; Parker, 1995).

Non-repudiation mechanisms prevent the receiver or the originator of e-commerce transactions from denying that the transaction was received or sent. Non-repudiation of origin protects the message receiver against the sender denying the message was sent. Non-repudiation of receipt protects the message sender from the receiver denying that the message was received (Dosdale, 1994; Jamieson, 1996; Marcella et al., 1998). Credibility can be quickly generated if appropriate feedback mechanisms on the Internet are implemented. Non-repudiation can be achieved by using the Secure Functional Acknowledgment Message (FUNACK) protocol.

Availability mechanisms provide legitimate access to e-commerce systems and deliver information only to authorized trading partners, when required, without any interruptions. Service level agreements specify hours of operations, maximum down time, and response time to maintain the availability of e-commerce systems. Disruptions to e-commerce systems can come from both natural and man-made disasters. These could lead to system breakdowns and errors. Inadvertent or deliberate corruption of e-commerce related applications could affect transactions, thereby impacting trading partner satisfaction, supplier relations, and perhaps business continuity. Availability issues are addressed by fault tolerance, duplication of communications links, and back-up systems that prevent denial of services to authorized trading partners (Marcella et al., 1998; Bhimani, 1996).

Access controls provide authorization mechanisms that aim to protect e-commerce messages against weaknesses (such as loss of messages) in the transmission media. They also protect sending trading partners against internal fraud or manipulation (Jamieson, 1996). Access control is achieved by implementing a secure operating system and segregating crucial e-commerce functions (such as inquiry, receipt, and payment) from unauthorized employees. In addition, implementing adequate and regular audit reviews and record retention procedures help to establish access controls (Marcella et al., 1998).

Best business practices are implemented to deter, prevent, detect, and recover quickly from risks in e-commerce by detecting suspicious activities. Best business practices include the extent and quality of top management commitment, written policies, procedures, standards, contingency measures, risk analysis, and management strategies. For example, Tallon et al. (2000) argue that "management practices" have an important role in the process of IT strategies intent towards a firm's performance, thus suggesting that best business practices can increase technology trust and ultimately, e-commerce

Table 10: Sub-concepts and definitions of technology trust mechanisms in e-commerce

Construct	Sub-Concepts	Definition
Technology Trust mechanisms in E-Commerce		Technology trust mechanisms in e-commerce are controls that provide assurances and guarantees in the form of security safeguards and protection services provided by e-commerce technologies, organizations, human, and third party services.
	Confidentiality	Protection of e-commerce transactions and message content against unauthorized reading, copying, or disclosure. Confidentiality examines the quality of encryption mechanisms and firewalls in e-commerce systems.
	Integrity	Assurance that e-commerce transactions have not been altered or deleted. Integrity examines the quality of audit procedures, sequencing of messages, and the existence of application and accounting controls.
	Authentication	Quality of being authoritative, valid, true, genuine, worthy of acceptance, or belief by reason of conformity to the fact that reality is present. Authentication examines the quality of the authorization mechanisms and acknowledgment procedures in use.
	Non-repudiation	Originators of e-commerce transactions cannot deny receiving or sending transactions. Non-repudiation examines the quality of acknowledgment and retention practices in place.
	Access controls	Protection of e-commerce transactions against weaknesses in the transmission media and protection of the sender against internal fraud or manipulation. Access controls examine the quality of the network access controls and authorization mechanisms in e-commerce.
	Availability	Assurance that e-commerce transactions are transmitted without interruption by providing authorized trading partners with an e-commerce system. Availability examines the segregation of duties and the security of the e-commerce networks.
	Best Business Practices	Refers to the policies, procedures, and standards that ensure the smooth functioning of e-commerce operations. Best business practices examine the extent and quality of top management commitment, written policies, procedures, contingency measures, risk analysis, and management strategies in place.

performance. Table 10 presents the sub-concepts and definitions of technology trust mechanisms.

OUTCOMES OF E-COMMERCE PARTICIPATION

The extent of e-commerce adoption in this study is measured by the extent to which an organization has adopted, integrated, and used e-commerce, and it is examined from two perspectives: first, the extent of e-commerce performance and second, the extent of trading partner relationship trust development.

Extent of e-commerce performance refers to the extent to which both trading partners perceive their relationship to be effective in realizing performance objectives. E-commerce performance is measured as a percentage of an organization's business using e-commerce, volume, and dollar value of the transactions. It is the mutually held trading partner perceptions and agreement of their sales performance and satisfaction.

Massetti and Zmud (1995) suggested that EDI adoption and diffusion could be classified into volume (number of document exchanges using EDI), diversity (number of distinct document types a company handles with its trading partners), breadth (number of established connections with external trading partners), and depth (degree of electronic consolidation between two or more trading partners).

Bensaou and Venkatraman (1996) suggest the importance of the "fit" between trust in the trading partners and the socio-political climate, which impacts the performance of inter-organizational systems. Similarly, electronic partnerships demand a conducive transaction climate and trust among trading partners (Anderson and Narus, 1990; Smith and Barclay, 1997). Hence, perceived e-commerce performance can be modeled as a predictor of satisfaction. Trading partners are likely to be more satisfied with relationships that are effective.

The extent of the development of trading partner trust relationships refer to the extent to which both trading partners in a relationship are satisfied with each other. The development of trust in trading partner relationships is measured by the intensity of communications, cooperation, and commitment, as well as increases in the number of trading partners. Trading partner satisfaction in e-commerce participation exists when trading partners are

Table 11: Sub-concepts and definitions of the outcomes of e-commerce participation

Construct	Sub-Concepts	Definition
Outcomes of E-Commerce Participation		Participation in e-commerce is the extent an e-commerce organization engages in the adoption, integration, and use of business-to-business e-commerce.
	Extent of E-Commerce Performance	Volume, dollar value, and types of business transactions exchanged between trading partners. Extent of e-commerce performance examines the volume and dollar value of e-commerce transactions.
	Extent of Trading Partner Trust relationship development	Positive affective state derived from all aspects of a trading partner relationship. Trading partner trust relationship development examines the cooperation, open communication, commitment, reputation, and long-term investments of trading partners.

engaged in long-term business investments, thereby leading to business continuity and improved reputations. In e-commerce, trading partner trust relationship development is based on:

- The degree of initial success each trading party had experienced in e-commerce participation,

- Well-defined roles for all trading parties,

- Realistic expectations, and

- A well-designed trading partner agreement, used as a guideline and not as a source of pressure.

Table 11 presents the sub-concepts and definitions of outcomes of e-commerce participation.

PERSPECTIVE OF ORGANIZATIONAL, ECONOMIC, AND POLITICAL THEORIES ON INTER-ORGANIZATIONAL TRUST

Limited research on inter-organizational trust within bi-directional dyads in e-commerce warrants interest in this topic. This study focused not only on the technological perspective, but also on the behavioral, economical, and political perspectives. Although many theories exist that are applicable to the diffusion of e-commerce technologies, inter-organizational-relationship theory (organizational theory), transaction-cost economics theory (economic dimension), and resource-dependency theory (political dimension) were used to examine trust in business relationships because they focused on trust-related behaviors in organizations. Analysis of these theories together with the findings of the exploratory study contributed to the development of the conceptual model.

Inter-Organizational-Relationship Theory and Trust Perspective

Inter-organizational relationship (IOR) theory focuses on reasons and conditions for forming relationships that include socio-political, structural, behavioral, and procedural dimensions (Oliver, 1990; Ring and Van de Ven, 1994; Van de Ven and Ferry, 1980). Inter-organizational relationships have been variously described as value-added partnerships (Henderson, 1990; Johnston and Vitale, 1988) derived from implementing information systems, inter-organizational information systems (IOS), (Cash and Konsynski, 1985; Johnston and Vitale, 1988), and electronic integration (Malone et al., 1987; Zaheer and Venkatraman, 1995). Inter-organizational relationship theory considers situational, structural, and procedural factors that are relevant for e-commerce participation.

(1) Situational factors describe reasons for forming inter-organizational relationships. These factors include resource necessity, procurement and allocation, political pressure, asymmetry or dependency, the legitimizing of current organizational operations, external efficiency opportunities, reciprocity, and resource predictability (Bensaou and Venkatraman, 1996; Reekers and Smithson, 1996; Van de Ven and Ferry, 1976).

(2) Structural factors refer to procedures and governance mechanisms that control e-commerce transactions and exchanges between trading partners. Structural factors form formal institutional arrangements and governance mechanisms that prescribe an overall pattern of interactions in inter-organizational-relationships. Formalization of these interactions refers to the extent to which rules, procedures, instructions, and communications are written (Pugh et al., 1968). It examines the extent of exchange resources and information administered through formal written policies, procedures, and contracts.

Vijayasarthy and Robey (1997) examined EDI adoption in smaller retailers, and they found that intensity, formalization, and information quality were important in dyadic relationships. Information quality was seen in the integrity of e-commerce transactions (accuracy, timeliness, speed, and completeness of e-commerce transactions). This study argues that although centrality (i.e., the extent to which resources and information flows are dominated by one or a few trading partners) was not found to be important, it may not be completely true in the case of EDI automotive manufacturers. The automotive industry was characterized by centrality of industry standards and coercive power exercised by large buyers pressuring smaller suppliers to adopt EDI (Helper, 1991; Webster, 1995).

(3) Procedural factors refer to the interactions and behaviours that arise from trading partner interdependencies. Interdependencies among trading partners may cause exchange behaviors such as power, dependence, cooperation, conflict, and trust, that affect the performance of inter-organizational relationships (Anderson and Narus, 1990; Ganesan, 1994; Kumar, 1996; Morgan and Hunt, 1994).

Inter-organizational relationship theory contributes to a useful approach of analyzing causes and conditions for forming trading partner relationships in e-commerce participation. In particular, inter-organizational relationships theory provides insights into e-commerce transactions, information flows, linkages, trading partner behaviours, interactions, and environmental factors (Bensaou and Venkatraman, 1996; Clemons et al., 1993; Malone et al., 1987; Oliver, 1990; Ring and Van de Ven, 1994; Van de Ven and Ferry, 1976).

Inter-organizational relationship theory has its limitations in that it fails to adequately distinguish between types of resources and organizations. The major limitation of previous studies in inter-organizational relationships is that they simply extended or adapted the study across organizational levels without articulating which distinct role the study addresses.

Transaction-Cost Economics Theory and Trust Perspective

Transaction-cost economics seeks to explain the economic rationale of alternative forms of organization, i.e., their relative efficiency. Williamson (1975) suggests that where transactions have highly uncertain outcomes, recur infrequently, and require unique or transaction-specific investment, they can be performed most efficiently within hierarchies.

Trading partners normally negotiate and monitor trading partner agreements as legal contracts to protect themselves from opportunistic behaviours and risks. Transaction costs are affected by asset specificity, uncertainties, complexity of exchange, bounded rationality, and behavioural factors such as opportunism.

Hill (1990) suggests it is possible to reduce transaction costs through a reputation for non-opportunistic behaviour. While it is difficult to observe the difference between opportunistic versus cooperative behaviours, it is possible to select cooperative trading partners. Opportunistic actions within a single market might yield short-term benefits, but there is a long-term cost: the lack of trust that results might inhibit future acquisitions of cost-reducing and/or quality-enhancing assets (Kumar, 1996). Trust is not purely an economic phenomenon that can be reduced to a calculation in cost/benefit terms. Trust can also be found in social relationships because "reputation has an economic value" (Hill, 1990).

Transaction-cost economics (TCE) contributes to an economic rationale understanding in the role of trading partner trust relationships. Williamson (1975) suggests that agents in any principal-agent relationship are not to be trusted and that the risk of opportunism is high. Williamson (1975:109) suggests that business managers often do act on the basis of trust but it is difficult to identify trustworthy agents. The concern is how to develop efficient safeguard strategies against the hazards of opportunism in the absence of uncertainty about the trading partner's trustworthiness. In addition, trust is an ongoing, market-oriented, economic calculation; its value is derived from results of creating and sustaining the relationship relative to the costs of maintaining or severing it. Hence, trust is critical, particularly when the economic value of trading partner relationships is in question.

The limitation of transaction-cost economics theory is that the traditional transaction cost approach ignores the role of inter-organizational relations for the purpose of development and exchange of resources and competencies. TCE theory assumes opportunism as standard behaviour. It ignores the crucial role that informal, socially embedded personal relationships have in producing stable relations of trust, obligation, and custom among formally independent organizations (Ring and Van de Ven, 1992). Transaction-cost economics does not make a universal claim that applies to all organizations, nor does it accurately predict what will happen in specific situations (Reekers and Smithson,

1996). In addition, transaction-cost economics provides limited insights into the strategic choices of organizations and their abilities to adopt particular technologies. It neglects both the political and other non-economic aspects of inter-organizational relationships.

Resource Dependency Theory and Trust Perspective

Resource dependency theory complements transaction-cost economics theory by adding a process dimension concerned with economic decision-making. It includes the political behavioural aspects of inter-organizational dyads (Pfeffer and Salancik, 1978; Reekers and Smithson, 1996). Resource dependency theory or political economy explicitly recognizes the political dimensions of the dyad. Resource dependency theory is concerned with:

- External forces in the prevailing and prospective environment within which the dyad operates; it accepts that members of the dyad are shaped by the internal structure and processes of the relationship through adaptation and interactions (Pfeffer and Salancik, 1978);

- Inter-organizational dimensions; and

- Interactions, as they influence the nature of the relationship within the dyad (Bensaou and Venkatraman, 1996).

Resource dependency theory contributes to political economic dimensions because of its holistic approach. It explicitly addresses the whole relationship over time; its history, anticipated future, and economic and political, as well as structural and behavioral, dimensions. Ganesan (1994) found that trust and dependence play key roles in determining the long-term orientation of inter-organizational relationships.

The limitation of resource dependency theory is that it lacks conceptual and operational definitions (Bensaou and Venkatraman, 1996; Reekers and Smithson, 1996). The previous section discussed inter-organizational relationship theory (organizational theory), transaction-cost economics theory (economic perspective), and resource dependency theory (political perspective). In the next section we discuss the evolution from inter-organizational systems to inter-organizational trust.

Evolution of Inter-Organizational Systems to Inter-Organizational Trust

E-commerce technologies and Information Technology (IT) have become the main tools for implementing business processes between organizations. Inter-Organizational Systems (IOS) refers to *"an automated information system shared by two or more companies"* implemented for efficient exchange of business transactions (Cash and Konsynski, 1985, p134). Inter-organizational-systems facilitate the exchange of information electronically across organizational boundaries and provide both processing capabilities and communication links. The potential for inter-organizational systems to serve as strategic information systems has been extensively discussed in academic journals (Cash and Konsynski, 1985; Johnston and Vitale, 1988). Inter-organizational systems facilitate the exchange of business transactions among trading partners, as they improve the speed, ease, and quality of information transfer. Through inter-organizational systems, buyers and sellers arrange routine exchanges of business transactions, sometimes without direct negotiations. Because information is exchanged over telecommunications networks using prearranged formats, there is minimal need for telephone calls, paper documents, or business correspondence to carry out the transactions. Value-added networks, Internet-based EDI systems, intranets, and extranet systems are examples of inter-organizational systems. IOS's are a direct result of the growing desire to interconnect business partners for the purpose of reducing costs by streamlining processes, collapsing cycle time, and eliminating inefficiencies associated with paper processing.

Trust can be placed by one individual (trading partner) or a group of individuals (trading partners) in an organization. Moreover, trading partners in an organization may share common orientation towards trading partners in another organization. Inter-organizational systems provide a basis for trading partners to coordinate and share information, which enhances competitive advantage (Arunachalam, 1997; Blois, 1999; Dyer and Chu, 2000; Zaheer et al., 1998). Consistent trading partner interactions between organizations lead to inter-organizational trust.

Organizational trust can be more transferable and can affect trading partners' responsibilities (Dow et al., 1998). Blois (1999) interprets inter-organizational trust as short hand for "two sets of individuals each of which is trusting the organization of which the others are members". In other words, an organization might rely on a particular supplier because of his/her proven technical competence and reputation for dealing fairly. However, the employees will be the ones who actually trust the supplier and determine whether or not the supplier is trustworthy. Doney and Cannon's (1997) study investigates the impact of supplier firm and salesperson trust on a buying firm's current supplier choice. They explicitly assume "persons and organizations can develop trust in a supplier firm's salesperson" (Doney and Cannon, 1997, p.35). Thus inter-organizational relationships from this perspective lead to inter-organizational trust because they describe the extent of employees' trust toward their trading partner's organization (Zaheer et al., 1998).

Table 12: A synthesis of theories applied in the conceptual model

Measurement Characteristics	IOR's Theory	TCE's Theory	Resource Dependency Theory	Trust in Business Relationships	Technology Trust Mechanisms in E-commerce
Paradigm	Social exchange theory Industrial marketing	Classical and neo-classical economics	Socio-political	Organizational behaviour	Diffusion of technology
Unit of Analysis	Dyadic inter-organizational-relationships	Relational transaction costs	Dyadic inter-organizational-relationships	Business relationships Buyer-seller Manufacturer-supplier	Trading partners
Basic Assumption	Inter-organizational-relations arise for a purpose and entail a particular set of structural, formal, and procedural dimensions	The transaction costs determine the choice of an optimal governance structure	The extent of dependence between trading partners	The extent of trading partner trust	The reliance on technology efficiencies
Strengths	Examines reasons for the formation of situational, structural, procedural, and behavioural dimensions of dyadic inter-organizational-relationships	Analyzes the efficiency and costs of governance structures	Considers political dimensions (imbalance of power, conflict resolution in an Inter-organizational-dyad (IOD)	Examines the extent an Inter-Organizational-dyad is willing to cooperate, share information, communicate, coordinate, and commit	Examines economic benefits from E-commerce systems and contributes to best business practices
Weaknesses	Determinants covered are broad ranging and heterogeneous. Previous studies focused primarily on public and welfare sector	Narrow focus on economic aspects. Discrete and static analysis which assumes the existence of an optimal structure	Lacks empirical research and a conceptual definition of its dimensions	Limited empirical research of inter-organizational trust in e-commerce participation	Only focuses on the technology. Business-to-business has taken off but is still in its early stages of growth in the Asia Pacific region.
Contribution to this study and Conceptual Model	Conceptualizes the reasons for formation, situational, structural, and behavioural exchanges in inter-organizational-relationships from an organizational perspective	Conceptualizes the efficiency of inter-organizational-dyadic relationships	Conceptualizes political dimensions of Inter-organizational-dyad relationships.	Analyzes antecedent trust factors that determine different types of inter-organizational trust and how trust affects e-commerce participation	Analyzes reasons for trust and security-based mechanisms Inter-organizational-dyads and how they affect e-commerce participation
Perspective	Organizational	Economic	Political	Behavioural	Technological

Sydow (1998:35) defines inter-organizational trust (IOT) as *"the confidence of an organization in the reliability of other organizations regarding a given set of outcomes or events."* As this study examines dyadic relationships, we adapt Sydow's definition and define inter-organizational trust as *"the confidence in the reliability of two organizations in a possibly risky situation that all trading partners involved in the action will act competently and dutifully."*

Thus, inter-organizational systems implemented for the sole purpose of e-commerce contributes to the development of inter-organizational relationships. Repeated daily interactions in inter-organizational relationships lead to the incremental development of inter-organizational trust.

Table 12 provides a summary of the theoretical perspectives applied in this chapter, together with the findings of the exploratory study. It forms the basis for the development of the conceptual model. The table highlights the basic assumptions, units of analysis, strengths, weaknesses, and contributions to the development of the conceptual model.

CONCEPTUAL MODEL OF INTER-ORGANIZATIONAL TRUST IN E-COMMERCE PARTICIPATION

The conceptual model was developed from the findings of the exploratory survey on the importance of trading partner trust and from theories in multiple disciplines including marketing, management, sociology, information systems, and e-commerce. Theoretical perspectives contributing to the development of the conceptual model include trust in business relationships, technology trust mechanisms in e-commerce, inter-organizational relationships (IOR's), transaction-cost economics (TCE), and resource-dependency theories. These theoretical perspectives yielded an understanding of the potential strengths and weaknesses of trading partner relationships in e-commerce participation. Moreover, they also provided a unique emphasis by not only considering the organizational, technological, economic, and socio-political perspectives of IOR's, but also the behavioral dimensions relating to interactions between trading partners in dyadic relationships. Figure 6 depicts the conceptual model of inter-organizational trust in e-commerce participation.

Figure 6: Conceptual model of inter-organizational trust in e-commerce participation

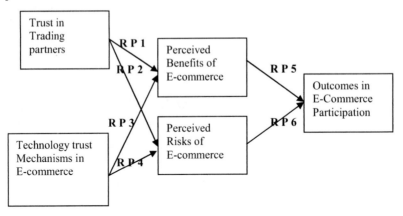

Table 13: Research propositions

R P 1: Trading partner trust is positively associated with perceived benefits of e-commerce.
R P 2: Trading partner trust is negatively associated with perceived risks of e-commerce.
R P 3: Technology trust mechanisms in e-commerce are positively associated with perceived benefits of e-commerce.
R P 4: Technology trust mechanisms in e-commerce are negatively associated with perceived risks of e-commerce.
R P 5: Perceived benefits of e-commerce are positively associated with e-commerce participation.
R P 6: Perceived risks of e-commerce are negatively associated with e-commerce participation.

Table 13 presents the research propositions. In the next section we justify the research propositions.

The Relationship between Trading Partner Trust and Perceived Benefits of E-Commerce

The proposed link between trading partner trust and perceived benefits of e-commerce is a subject of much discussion among researchers who have studied trust in business relationships and organizations (Barney and Hansen, 1994; Cummings and Bromiley, 1996; Doney and Cannon, 1997; McAllister, 1995; Mishra, 1996; Morgan and Hunt, 1994; Kumar, 1996; Ring and Van de Ven, 1994). A variety of research and evidence suggests that there is a positive relationship between trust and benefits.

Competence trust demonstrates a trading partner's ability and skills to operate business-to-business e-commerce applications. Consistent positive role competence contributes to the development of credibility among trading partners. When trading partners are able to send and receive e-commerce transactions correctly and in a timely manner, they are contributing to economic benefits derived from time and cost savings and from avoiding re-training or requesting trading partners to re-send the same transaction correctly.

Credibility from a series of consistent positive competence trust promotes reliability and willingness of trading partners to trust each other and value their relationship, thereby making them predictable and trustworthy. Predictability trust in turn increases trading partners' confidence and encourages them to share information (i.e., timely, accurate, honest, and relevant). Trading partners exhibit collaboration, cooperation, communication openness, and satisfaction, which contribute to relationship-related benefits. Morgan and Hunt (1994) conducted a study of distribution channels and found that high levels of cooperation among trading partners contributed to satisfaction. Cooperation reduces conflict, increases communication and trading partner satisfaction and capitalizes on relationship-related benefits (Anderson and Narus, 1990; Morgan and Hunt, 1994). Satisfaction in turn reinforces trading partner trust and reduces the probability of trading partners behaving opportunistically, thereby inhibiting relationship-related risks (such as cheating, lying, or giving inaccurate information). Moreover, satisfaction also increases commitment among trading partners and encourages long-term trading partner relationships and increased participation in e-commerce. Trading partners then gradually move to capitalize on the strategic benefits of e-commerce (Anderson and Weitz, 1989; Ganesan, 1994; Morgan and Hunt, 1994).

As predictability trust gradually develops into goodwill trust, trading partners experience strategic benefits derived from improved reputation and image of their organizations. Empirical evidence supports the link between suppliers' reputation and buyers' trust (Doney and Cannon, 1997; Ganesan, 1994). For example, in a study of industrial channel dyads, a retailer's favorable perception of its vendor's reputation led to increased credibility and trust (Ganesan, 1994). Goodwill trust is an important ingredient for long-term trading partner relationships because it shifts the focus to future conditions and encourages trading partners to increase investments in e-commerce participation (Anderson and Weitz, 1989; Dwyer, Schurr, and Oh, 1987; Morgan and Hunt, 1994). Therefore, we propose that:

R-P 1: Trading partner trust is positively associated with perceived benefits of e-commerce.

The Relationship between Trading Partner Trust and Perceived Risks of E-Commerce

The literature on trust suggests that regardless of the analysis level, trading partners remain vulnerable to some extent (Doney and Cannon, 1997; Williamson, 1975). Ring and Van de Ven (1994) and Das and Teng (1996) classified risks as either performance risks derived from the technology or relational risks derived from trading partner relationships. Interdependencies between trading partners can cause task uncertainties that contribute to technology performance-related risks derived from incompatible systems. Furthermore, uncertainties may be derived from poor business practices or a lack of competence trust due to changes in e-commerce applications in the operating environment.

Similarly, a situation of imbalance of power between trading parties permits one of the trading partners to exercise coercive power and exhibit opportunistic behaviours with respect to the other (Hart and Saunders, 1997; Helper, 1991; Hill, 1990). Examples of coercive power used by powerful buyers in the automotive industry may include: slow delivery of vehicles to their distributors, slow payment on warranty work, unfair distribution of vehicles, threat of termination, and bureaucratic red tape (Webster, 1995). A situation of imbalance of power can create mistrust among trading partners. Furthermore, an exercise of coercive power among trading partners can motivate a lack of cooperation, encourage conflicts among trading partners, and contribute to a lack of goodwill trust. In addition, a dissatisfied trading partner will be suspicious of the other trading partner's intentions and motives and will demonstrate reluctance to share and engage in open communications, thus leading to general risks. Hill (1990) suggests that a lack of trust affects the reputation of trading partners, and has an economic cost.

A series of consistent negative behaviours derived from a lack of cooperation and the absence of collaboration or prior consensus about the structure, function, and design of e-commerce networks may lead to predictability mistrust. In the long run, this can lead to fewer opportunities for smaller trading partners to develop their knowledge and expertise of e-commerce use, thus contributing to relational risks.

While opportunistic behaviours among trading partners derived from poor business practices may yield short-term benefits, the long-term costs from a lack of goodwill trust among trading partners inhibit future acquisitions of cost-reducing and/or quality-enhancing assets (Kumar, 1996). Therefore, we propose that:

R-P 2: Trading partner trust is negatively associated with perceived risks of e-commerce.

The Relationship between Technology Trust Mechanisms in E-Commerce and Perceived Benefits of E-Commerce

The proposed link between technology trust mechanisms in e-commerce and their impact on perceived benefits has been studied by researchers who examined security services in e-commerce. Technology trust mechanisms are mostly derived from e-commerce technologies, third party services, and organizations (as in human/actors). By human actors we mean auditors, security analysts, and top management personnel who are committed to enforcing best business practices in their organization. For example, the implementation of encryption mechanisms and the automation of e-commerce technologies can prevent transactions from being intercepted, manipulated, or deleted and leads to accurate, complete, correct, and timely business transactions. This, in turn, contributes to economic benefits of savings in time and costs (Dearing, 1990). For example, Mukhopadhyay, Kekre, and Kalathur (1995) conducted a study of nine Chrysler assembly centers and found that EDI improved the quality of information exchanged, and reduced inventory, transportation, and administrative costs. They concluded that over a ten-year period, EDI use had helped Chrysler to realize a benefit of over $100 per vehicle, thus amounting to annual savings of $200 million. Therefore, the speed and automation provided by e-commerce technologies enable trading partners to not only achieve accurate, timely information, but also to increase their productivity and profitability (Nath et al., 1998; Premkumar et al., 1997; Senn, 2000).

Similarly, functional acknowledgments in the form of email feedbacks or other e-commerce protocols providing reliable and timely feedback mechanisms that increase trading partner satisfaction contributes to relationship-related benefits. For example, each trading partner has a reference (sequence) number that identifies where the transaction came from and contributes to accurate information. E-commerce applications thus enable product and service differentiation and establish tighter links with suppliers, distributors, and customers (trading partners). Consequently, both trading partners and customers achieve relationship-related benefits such as customer satisfaction and competitive advantages.

Top management commitment enforces audit, contingency planning procedures. The existence of top management commitment can also encourage trading partners to abide by best business practices. This strengthens a trading partner's reputation for exercising high standards, quality, and fairness, and contributes to strategic benefits where trading partners commit to long-term investments. Therefore, we propose that:

R-P 3: Technology trust mechanisms in e-commerce are positively associated with perceived benefits of e -commerce.

The Relationship between Technology Trust Mechanisms in E-Commerce and Perceived Risks of E-Commerce

A lack of technology trust mechanisms in e-commerce may introduce vulnerabilities that make e-commerce a risky course of action (Hart and Saunders, 1997; Marcella et al., 1998). For example, a denial of service attack can occur when a malicious party (internal or external) cripples the network server's ability to respond to requests, (usually by flooding the server with many requests), or an organization may encounter software deliberately infected by a virus. These threats contribute to technology performance-related risks. Unauthorized access to e-commerce systems may provide increased opportunities for malicious parties to modify the records of single organizations or of their trading partners (Marcella et al., 1998; Parker, 1995). Such unauthorized modifications and deletions of e-commerce transactions may lead to integrity issues. Trading partners may act on those messages assuming that they came from a genuine authorized trading partner, which can contribute to technology performance-related risks and relational risks.

Similarly, poor business practices such as lack of proper training, inadequate audit and back-up retention policies and procedures, or poor contingency planning procedures, can lead to general risks. For example, the costs associated with businesses due to unavailable servers can severely impact business if real-time transactions are involved. Inadvertent or deliberate corruption of e-commerce records could impact trading partner satisfaction and perhaps the ultimate business continuity. Therefore, we propose that:

R-P 4: Technology trust mechanisms in e-commerce are negatively associated with perceived risks of e-commerce.

The Relationship between Perceived Benefits and Participation in E-Commerce

Trading partner trust and perceived benefits of e-commerce contribute to increased participation in e-commerce. For example, e-commerce technologies provide speed and automation of business processes, which reduces transaction and administrative costs and contributes to direct (economic) benefits. Consequently, e-commerce applications provide real-time tracking information where buyers can log into the supplier's extranet application, track shipment details, and estimate arrival dates of goods they ordered (Riggins and Rhee, 1998; Senn, 2000).

Buyers are able to satisfy their end customers' needs by delivering the goods on time and increasing their customer satisfaction, and that in turn contributes to relationship-related benefits. Increased satisfaction from e-commerce performance contributes to high levels of predictability and goodwill trading partner trust. A series of consistent, high-quality services capitalizes on strategic benefits. Strategic benefits include long-term investments (as in increased volume, diversity, and dollar value of e-commerce transactions), and increased reputation of organizations (Anderson and Narus, 1990; Doney and Cannon, 1997; Kumar, 1996; Morgan and Hunt, 1994; Smith and Barclay, 1997). For example, evidence of such trust-based performance was found by comparing supplier relationships in the automotive industry in Japan and United States. It was found that Toyota's relationship with its suppliers was deeply embedded in long-standing networks of social and economic relations characterized by high levels of goodwill trust, thus contributing to perceived economic, relationship-related, and strategic benefits (Barney and Hansen, 1994). Therefore, we propose that:

R-P 5: Perceived benefits of e-commerce are positively associated with participation in e-commerce.

The Relationship between Perceived Risks and Participation in E-Commerce

Participation in e-commerce involves time and costs. Trading partners may be operating with incompatible systems that lack security mechanisms. This may give rise to technology performance-related risks, an incompatible infrastructure, and loss in the transmission media, thus restricting participation in e-commerce (Jamieson, 1996).

Trading partners (as in suppliers) who make sacrifices and show concern for other trading partners (who could be their retailers and manufacturers) develop a reputation for fairness within their industry. Consistent behaviours from trading partners provide signals of their future actions. On the other hand, vendors who have a reputation for terminating relationships and seeking high profits provide signals to their retailers that they are solely interested in their own profits, thus contributing to relational risks that restrict participation in e-commerce (Helper, 1991; Langfield-Smith and Greenwood, 1998; Webster, 1995).

Similarly, trading partners who found themselves participating in inequitable relationships felt angry and resentful. Such feelings of dissatisfaction may result in suspicion, mistrust, and conflicts. Trading partners may view each other as untrustworthy and exploitative. Consequently, trading partners will not trust each other and will not commit to long-term trading partner relationships. This inhibits e-commerce participation and contributes to relational risks and general risks (Dwyer et al., 1987; Ganesan, 1994; Smith and Barclay, 1997). Poor business practices and mistrust among trading partners thus contribute to general risks of e-commerce. Therefore, we propose that:

R-P 6: Perceived risks in e-commerce are negatively associated with participation in e-commerce.

This chapter examined and discussed trust from multi-disciplinary perspectives. Previous models of trust in business relationships were examined in order to identify trust behaviours and characteristics. Trust in inter-organizational relationships (IOR), transaction-cost economics (TCE), and resource dependency theories were analyzed in order to provide an organizational, economic, and socio-political perspective of trust in e-commerce participation. Technology trust mechanisms in e-commerce were examined, which led to security principles that provided a technology perspective in e-commerce. Further, perceived benefits (strengths) and perceived risks (weaknesses) of e-commerce determined the extent of inter-organizational trust in e-commerce participation. Then, we discussed the evolution of inter-organizational systems to inter-organizational and the development of a conceptual model. Finally, we presented the definitions of the constructs and sub-concepts in the conceptual model and justified the research propositions. The next chapter will describe the research process and justify the multiple case study research method selected to test the conceptual model.

Chapter IV

Research Method

In chapter 3, we reviewed the current literature from theories in multi-disciplines leading to the development of the conceptual model of inter-organizational trust in e-commerce participation. In this chapter, we first discuss different research methods in information systems followed by analysis of quantitative and qualitative research approaches. Then we provide the reasons for selecting a case study research method followed by a description of the research process, design, and instrumentation of the conceptual model, leading to a semi-structured questionnaire, data collection, and data analysis procedures that take into consideration the validity of data.

RESEARCH METHODS IN INFORMATION SYSTEMS

Several researchers emphasize the importance of identifying the epistemological and philosophical foundation of research (Galliers, 1992; Klein and Myers, 1999; Neuman, 1994). Galliers (1992) makes a distinction between research method and research approach. He suggests that a research approach is the way of going about one's research, and may utilize different research methods and techniques. He classifies research approaches into two categories: a "positivist" and an "interpretivist" research approach, as shown in Table 14. Each technique makes an underlying philosophical assumption about the purpose of science and the nature of social reality.

Positivist research philosophy presupposes that reality exists independently of the researcher and suggests that it can be objectively and rigorously measured.

Interpretivist philosophy asserts that reality is a construct that people apply, and that social phenomenon cannot be examined independently of the individuals contributing to that reality. It also suggests that researchers themselves cannot be totally objective. It is from the researcher's conceptual orientation that the research questions, interpretations, and explanations flow (Galliers, 1992). Consequently, interpretative research emphasizes the context of this research and specifies the need for critical reflections on social and historical background of the research setting.

Based on these two types of philosophies, choosing the right research method becomes even more important. A wide variety of Information Systems

Table 14: Common research approaches used in information systems research

Positivist	Interpretivst
Surveys	Subjective/Argumentative Reviews
Case Studies	Case Studies
Laboratory Experiments	Action Research (descriptive/interpretive)
Field Experiments	Future research
Theorem Proof	Role/game playing
Forecasting	
Simulation	

Table 15: Research questions and types of research strategies

Strategy	Form of research question?	Requires control over behavior and events?	Focuses on contemporary events?
Experiment	How? Why?	Yes	Yes
Survey	Who? What? Where? How many? How much?	No	Yes
Archival analysis	Who? What? Where? How many? How much?	No	Yes/No
History	How? Why?	No	No
Case Study	How? Why?	No	Yes

research methods and their links to other reference disciplines (such as business, humanities, social sciences, management, and marketing) have made the choice of a research method even more complex. Yin (1994, p 6) suggests that choosing a research method requires a thorough understanding of the nature of the research question to be answered, as well as the characteristics of the method designed to provide the answer. Table 15 presents the different types of research questions in relation to the research method adapted from Yin (1994).

Furthermore, Yin (1994) suggests that apart from understanding the nature and purpose of existing research methods, it is important to address the following three questions when considering an appropriate research method:

(1) The type of research question posed is addressed. This study examines "how" and "why" types of research questions, such as how does inter-organizational trust (trading partner trust) influence the perception of benefits and risks of e-commerce, thus influencing the extent of participation in e-commerce?

(2) The extent of control an investigator has over the actual behavioural events should be considered. The investigator (researcher) in this study had no control over the actual behaviour of the trading partners and events.

(3) The degree of focus on contemporary, as opposed to historical, events should be considered. In this study, the focus on contemporary events was high, as trust in business-to-business e-commerce on the Internet was a relatively new phenomenon.

This study focused on how and why research questions in a natural setting because the concept of inter-organizational trust was new in the Information Systems discipline when this study was initiated.

QUANTITATIVE AND QUALITATIVE RESEARCH APPROACHES

Interest in qualitative research methods is growing in IS research (Klein and Myers, 1999). Despite the dominance of positivism, there are signs that interpretivism is gaining ground, and the epistemological choice between interpretivism and positivism is becoming an important issue for IS researchers (Walsham, 1995). The following section briefly describes both these approaches.

The *quantitative approach* implies that an objective truth exists in the outside world, and this truth can be revealed through scientific methods for measuring and analyzing relationships among different variables systematically and statistically. The major concerns in quantitative methodology are that the measurements are reliable, valid, and generalizable in their predictions of cause and effect.

Quantitative methods attempt to use standardized measures so that various perspectives and experiences of people can be fit into a standard set of categories. The advantage of quantitative research is that it is possible to obtain and present a broad generalized set of findings concisely and succinctly. Hence, the focus is on the validation of the measuring instrument (for example, a survey) where a larger population receives the questionnaire.

Qualitative research approaches cover an array of interpretative techniques that seek to describe, decode, translate, and otherwise come to terms with the meaning, rather than the frequency, of naturally occurring phenomena in the social world. Recently, in IS research, there has been a shift from the quantitative paradigm to the qualitative paradigm (see Klein and Myers, 1999). Researchers who once saw statistical analysis as rigorous and reliable now argue that subjectivity (for example, in the case study research method) has added strength to qualitative researchers (Yin, 1994). Qualitative methods allow researchers to study selected issues in depth without being restricted by predetermined categories of analysis. Silverman (1998) suggests that the particular strength of qualitative research for both researchers and practitioners is its ability to focus on actual practice in situ (i.e., looking at how organizations are routinely enacted).

Qualitative techniques emerge from phenomenology and interpretative paradigms that emphasize a constructive approach, which assumes no clear-cut objectivity or reality. A case study is a specific method or technique within the research applied in interpretivism. A case study may involve a detailed study of a single organization (single case study) or group of organizations (multiple case studies). Case studies explore, describe, or explain in detail a particular issue within a unit of study (Benbasat et al., 1987; Yin, 1994). The data from case studies are useful for their qualitative richness normally obtained in a complex and real world situation.

Qualitative data reveals participants' thoughts and words during the interviews and conversations. This allows the researcher to better assess the meanings people place on their experiences, perceptions, and assumptions in their surrounding social world. Hence, the word *qualitative* implies an emphasis on the processes and meanings that cannot be examined or measured in terms of quantity, amount, intensity, or frequency. Social and organizational life is perceived as emerging from the shared creativity of individuals. Furthermore, qualitative researchers produce a great deal of information about a smaller set of cases, thus increasing their in-depth understanding of the cases. Hence, the use of qualitative research stresses the socially constructed nature of reality.

Myers (1994) suggests that the distinguishing feature of qualitative research is the focus on a few entities (e.g., people, organizations, and systems) in depth, rather than many entities more selectively. There are a variety of qualitative research methods, including the case study research strategy, the grounded theory approach, ethnography, semonitics, hermeneutics, longitudinal/historical studies, and action research. These research approaches differ in their purposes, procedures, and evaluation criteria.

Qualitative researchers propose the use of a triangulation of methods as one way to achieve rigor during data collection. Using multiple methods (or triangulation) secures an in-depth understanding of the phenomena in question. Triangulation is not a tool or strategy of validation, but rather an alternative to validation. The combination of multiple perspectives, methods, empirical materials, and observations in a study is therefore best understood as a strategy adding rigor, breadth, and depth to any investigation.

JUSTIFICATION OF A CASE STUDY RESEARCH METHOD

Benbasat et al. (1987) suggest three justifications for a case study research method. Case study research method was selected in this study for the following reasons:

(1) A case study research approach (method) permits a study of inter-organizational-systems or information systems within their natural setting

and allows learning from the "state-of-the-art" practice. It permits generation of theories from practice.

(2)   A case study research approach (method) enables an understanding of the nature and complexity of processes occurring, by answering *how* and *why* research questions (Yin, 1994). Similarly, Walsham (1993) suggests that case studies are often advocated for intensive research, such as this, where we need to develop an in-depth understanding of the importance of inter-organizational trust in e-commerce participation.

(3)   Case study research approach (method) is an appropriate research method, especially in an area where few previous studies have been conducted, and where the study relates to contemporary events. Bonoma (1985) proposed that case research methods are useful when a "phenomenon is broad and complex, where the existing body of knowledge is insufficient to permit the posing of causal questions, and when a phenomenon cannot be studied outside the context in which it occurs" (Bonoma, 1985, p 199). Previous research on inter-organizational trust in e-commerce was limited (Hart and Saunders, 1997; Sako, 1998; Senn, 1998; Smeltzer, 1997). The concept of trust in e-commerce was not widely recognized or understood when this research was initiated. In fact it was hardly mentioned in the academic literature or practitioner journals. Studying inter-organizational trust in the business-to-business e-commerce participation phenomenon requires real organizations using e-commerce systems or operating in an e-commerce environment, and is therefore a complex area of study. Hence, the case study method was seen as relevant and appropriate for this study.

The potential strength of case studies include capturing *reality* in greater detail with the ability to analyze many variables, thus providing a richness of information about the situation or organization (Galliers, 1992). A semi-structured questionnaire comprising questions for the constructs in the conceptual model was designed to collect rich qualitative data. This study examined inter-organizational trust and its impact on perceived benefits, risks, and technology trust mechanisms in e-commerce, thereby influencing outcomes in e-commerce participation.

MULTIPLE CASE STUDIES

This study used multiple case studies, as it was considered to be an appropriate method chosen to test the research propositions (Yin, 1994). Yin suggests that: *"multiple case designs have distinct advantages and disadvantages in comparison to single case designs ... a major insight is to consider multiple cases as one would consider multiple experiments – that is, to follow a 'replication' logic. This is far different from a mistaken analogy in the past, which incorrectly considered multiple cases to be similar to the multiple respondents in a survey (or to the multiple subjects within an experiment) – that is to follow a sampling logic."* (Yin, 1989, 51)

Similarly, Benbasat, Goldstein, and Mead (1987) provided a clear rationale for using multiple case studies:

> Multiple case designs are desirable when the intent of the research is descriptive, theory building, or theory testing... Multiple case designs allow for cross case analysis and extension of theory. Of course, multiple cases yield more general research results. (Benbasat et al., 1987, 373)

Multiple case studies were chosen because they allowed an in-depth analysis of the concept in a real life situation, thus enabling trust behaviours and trading partner interactions to be observed. The conceptual model was tested in eight organizations (uni-directional dyads) that formed four bi-directional dyads from a cross section of industries. The organizations consisted of both large and small-medium enterprises, and public and private sector organizations. Some used simple applications (i.e., electronic applications without the Web) while others used more Web-based electronic applications and e-commerce technologies. This paved the way for a cross-case analysis of the findings and contributed to meaningful generalizations.

CASE STUDY RESEARCH DESIGN

A research design is a technical plan (distinguished from a management plan, which deals with resources, logistics, scheduling and assignment of personnel, and other tasks involved in administering a research project). It attempts to link the beginning and ending of a study, thus helping researchers to get "from here to there" (Yin, 1989).

According to Yin (1994), the following components make up a case study research design:

- Case study's questions using how and why types of questions. This study seeks to investigate and examine the importance of inter-organizational trust in e-commerce participation within a natural setting. The research question developed for this study is: How does inter-organizational trust (trading partner trust) influence the perception of e-commerce benefits and risks of e-commerce, thus influencing the extent of participation in e-commerce? Furthermore, the dimensions/variables that examine the constructs and test the conceptual model are designed to include how and why types of questions as well. Examples of these questions include: "How do the ability and skills of your trading partner impact trust in your trading partners? Why is it so important for a trading partner to correctly send business-to-business transactions? Please provide an example of a successful situation and an unsuccessful situation. How did it occur and how did it impact the trust in your trading partner?"

- Research propositions direct the researcher to focus on what kinds of information to collect. Without research propositions the researcher might be tempted to collect everything.

- Unit of analysis. It is important to link the objectives and questions to a basic unit of analysis. The primary unit of analysis in this study is a directional dyad (i.e., an organization). The next level of analysis is the bi-directional dyad, which involves two organizations interacting with each other. Ideally the concept of trust would be examined from both parties within a bi-directional dyad. By its very nature trust implies two parties, a subject A – the trusting party (trustor) and an object of trust B – the trusted party (trustee). Hence, the unit of analysis in this study is either the uni-directional dyad or two organizations forming a bi-directional dyad as shown in Figure 7. Organization A is part of a uni-directional dyad when it interacts with and trusts organization B.

In this study a bi-directional dyad involves both organizations A and B interacting and observing each other's trust. Hence, in one instance organization A is the trustor, and organization B is the trusted party, and in another

Figure 7: Uni and bi-directional dyads

Uni-directional dyad   **Bi-directional dyad**

instance the reverse takes place (i.e., organization B is the trustor and organization A is the trusted party).

• Logic of linking the data to the propositions. Multiple case studies paved the way for both qualitative and quantitative analysis of the data collected. One method used to link the data and propositions of this study is via pattern matching across cases (Yin, 1994, 25). Since the objective of this study was to achieve a better understanding of the importance of inter-organizational trust in e-commerce participation, a cross-referencing method was applied. Based on the responses from preliminary research, the semi-structured questionnaire was refined.

• The criteria for interpreting the findings should be directly related to ways of linking data and propositions of study (Yin, 1994, 25). Interpretation of the findings was carried out via pattern matching and explanation building (as in narrative descriptions and causal explanations). This led to analytic generalizations that created a story line and allowed predictions to be made. The first step identified recurring patterns and themes from the data collected during the interviews. Then the similarities and differences between the participants were identified. This was followed by a cross-case analysis of the cases that enabled generalizations to be made.

SAMPLING

The criteria applied for choosing the case studies (sampling) were as follows:

• Organizations should be actively engaged in business-to-business e-commerce;

• The participants who were interviewed for this study should be well versed in their business-to-business e-commerce operations and adoption procedures. They included e-commerce coordinators, IT managers, accounting managers, chief executive officers, security analysts, sales consultants, and intranet administrators;

• The participants in the organization should be willing to introduce the researcher to their other trading partner, thus enabling the researcher to examine both trading partners within a bi-directional dyad;

• Although only two uni-directional dyads (two organizations) participated within each bi-directional dyad, the interactions between the two organizations may include one-to-one trading partner relationships, one-to-many trading partner relationships, many-to-one trading partner relationships, or many-to-many. In this study the relationship between the bi-directional dyads was one-to-many, and many-to-many trading partner relationships. However, from these one-to-many, and many-to-many relationships only instances of dyadic relationships were extracted for study;

• The trading partners from both organizations should have met face-to-face at least once during the initial stages of e-commerce adoption (for example, to negotiate and write up trading partner agreements). This study gives priority to trading partners' behaviors and interactions rather than e-commerce technologies.

Finally, information about organizational product and background was gathered through document analysis. Due to time and budgetary constraints all the eight organizations that participated in this study were located in the Wellington region (in New Zealand). Entry into sites was obtained by making initial telephone calls to key representatives in the e-commerce organizations. A brief description and purpose of the study was discussed over the telephone before requesting them to participate. The telephone conversation was followed by an email including an attached file describing the purpose of the study. Most of the participants indicated their interest in participating in the study and requested that a report containing aggregate findings of all cases be given to them at the end of the study. Participants who were not interested in participating cited reasons such as immature use of e-commerce.

Once confirmation was received, appointment dates for interview sessions were arranged. Subjects were requested to answer structured and open-ended questions using a semi-structured questionnaire. The interview sessions were recorded, and participants verified and confirmed their responses through a draft report. Each organization that participated received a report of the final findings and a thank-you note.

Size of Research Sample

Galliers (1992) suggests that a single case study is useful when developing or refining generalizable concepts and frames of reference, but warned of the difficulty involved in generalizing. On the other hand, multiple case studies solved that problem. Yin (1994) suggests that a single case study is appropriate when it characterizes the critical case in testing a well-formulated theory. The theory identifies a clear set of propositions, as well as the circumstances within which the propositions were believed to be true. In this study, inter-organizational trust was still a relatively new phenomenon in e-commerce participation, and since no single case could hope to characterize the theory completely, a multiple case study research approach was deemed appropriate. Although multiple case studies permit a cross-case analysis and extension of theory, they also demand widespread resources and time (Benbasat et al., 1987; Yin, 1994). In order to limit the scope of the study to the time frame for completion, four bi-directional dyads consisting of eight organizations were chosen for this study.

Sampling Procedures (Choice of Organizations or Cases)

Galliers (1992) suggests that a sampling procedure must adequately represent the unit of analysis. The organizations that participated in this study were selected on the basis of having been involved in e-commerce for a substantial period of time, as shown in Table 16. For each organization in this study, an "object of trust" was also identified, thereby establishing a directional dyad of trust. Our sample included both uni and bi-directional dyads. Whereas in uni-directional dyads the phenomenon was examined only from one organization's perspective, in bi-directional dyads, reciprocal trust (i.e., trust from two directions) was examined.

In-depth case analyses were conducted in eight uni-directional dyads from a cross-section of industries, grouped to form four bi-directional dyads. The organizations included a public sector firm involved in customs clearance, their Internet service provider, a customs agent (broker), an importer, two organi-

Table 16: Summary of the uni-directional dyads that participated in this study

Organizations that participated in this study	Name of organization	Main role and size of the organization	Type of industry	No. of Respondents	Type of E-commerce Application
Bi-directional Dyad A Uni-directional Dyad 1	NZ Customs → Internet Service Provider	Provides Customs clearance service Large	Public service	10	CusMod using EDI X25 and other means via ISP
Bi-directional Dyad A Uni-directional Dyad 2	Internet Service Provider → NZ Customs	E-commerce services Small-Medium Enterprise (SME)	Internet service provider	2	Facilitates CusMod
Bi-directional Dyad B Uni-directional Dyad 3	Customs broker → Importer	Trade facilitator SME	Customs brokerage	2	Trade Manager using Visual Basic – Microsoft
Bi-directional Dyad B Uni-directional dyad 4	Importer → Customs broker	Retailing SME	Retailing and service	2	Trade Manager using Visual Basic – Microsoft
Bi-directional Dyad C Uni-directional dyad 5	Cisco NZ → Compaq NZ	Supplier SME	Computer and data communications	10	Extranet Cisco Connection online
Bi-directional Dyad C Uni-Directional Dyad 6	Compaq NZ → Cisco NZ	Buyer Large	Computer and data communications	4	Extranet Cisco Connection online
Bi-directional Dyad D Uni-directional Dyad 7	Siemens NZ → Telecom NZ	Supplier SME		4	Extranet Main stream Express
Bi-directional Dyad D Uni-directional Dyad 8	Telecom NZ → Siemens NZ	Buyer Large	Telecommunications	2	Extranet Main Stream Express

zations in the computer and data communications industries, and two organizations in the telecommunications industry.

DATA COLLECTION

Data collection refers to the logic of linking the data and the propositions. Yin (1994) identifies six sources of case study evidence. They include documentation, archival records, interviews, direct observation, participant-observation, and physical artifacts. Hence, the method used for data collection is significant, as it affects the quality of data collected. This study followed three principles in the data collection process. They include using multiple sources, maintaining a chain of evidence, and examining a variety of documents from the case.

- First, the use of multiple sources of evidence was seen as a major strength in the case study research method. For example, document analysis in our case included trading partner agreements, organization charts, web-sites, internal security policies giving evidence of the organization's best business practices, and their product information and background. In addition, trading procedures, answers to the semi-structured interview questionnaire, case study written notes, recorded audiotapes, and telephone interview written notes were used to collect data. Furthermore, document analysis, tabular materials, narrative descriptions of written candid conversations, and informal discussions held with participants also contributed to the case study database.

  The fieldwork proceeded in the following manner. The questionnaire was first pre-tested with a group of academics and e-commerce practitioners via e-mail and telephone interviews. The aim of pre-testing the semi-structured questionnaire was to refine the jargon (commercial language) to suit case sites and to ensure that the questions were adequately covered in order to test trading partner trust relationships (bi-directional dyads) in e-commerce participation. Questions were pre-structured to have a qualitative focus using how and why questions. In addition, participants provided examples and evidence of their responses. This later led to quantitative measures examining the impact levels of trust, technology trust mechanisms, perceived benefits, and risks that determined the extent

of e-commerce participation using likert scales (Low (0-3), Medium (4-6), and High (7-10)).
The semi-structured questionnaire included the following themes:

– Background information about the case, as in business processes and functions, and business-to-business e-commerce transactions roles/interactions;

– Trading partner trust relationships;

– Technology trust mechanisms in e-commerce;

– Perceived benefits of e-commerce;

– Perceived risks of e-commerce; and

– Extent of e-commerce participation.

• Second, maintaining a chain of evidence in order to increase the reliability of the data collected was important.

• Third, evidence for the case studies came from the written interview notes and telephone interview notes conducted to clarify the data collected during the interviews. In addition to the interviews, analysis of existing documents that related to e-commerce adoption, day-to-day interactions, internal security policies, and trading partner agreements were observed and analyzed. Hence, triangulation aimed to establish rigor and reflect an attempt to secure an in-depth understanding of inter-organizational trust in e-commerce participation.

Ensuring the Validity of Data

The validity of a case study research relies heavily on the sampling criteria, research process, the method of analysis, and interpretation of the data collected (Yin, 1994). Similarly, Benbasat et al. (1987) found unit of analysis, representatives of the sample, and inclusion of extreme examples to be important. In order to achieve a correct unit of analysis and obtain a representative sample to help identify extreme cases, the focus on the research question and objectives of this study was taken into consideration.

Table 17: Measures applied in data quality

Criteria	Approaches to achieving criteria	Phase of Empirical Research
Construct Validity	Use of multiple sources of evidence	Data Collection
	Establish chain of evidence	Data Collection
Internal Validity	Use of pattern matching	Data Analysis
	Use of cognitive mapping	Data Analysis
	Use of cluster analysis	Data Analysis
	Use of factor analysis	Data Analysis
External Validity	Perform multiple case studies	Research Design
		Case Selection
Reliability	Developing case study data base	Data Collection

The question of validity was achieved by applying credibility and generalizability of data and by simply seeking to describe the findings by providing a narrative account of the *thinking aloud* process and understanding how people make sense of their world. The quality of data collected in this study was maintained by following the criteria as suggested by Yin (1994) in Table 17.

The purpose of the semi-structured questionnaire is to test the research propositions in the conceptual model and the quality of data collected by this instrument was assured by the following means.

Construct validity aims to establish the correct operational measures for the concepts being studied (Yin, 1994, p 40). The lessons learned from the exploratory pilot case studies provided insights for improving and refining the semi-structured questionnaire used in the multiple case studies. In addition, construct validity was achieved by using multiple sources of evidence. Multiple sources of evidence contributed to "multiple measures of the same phenomenon". For example, wherever possible, more than one participant was interviewed in the organizations participating in this study. In addition, several documents related to the organization's background, products, and best business practices were examined. Moreover, key informants were asked to review the case study report. Yin (1984, p 139) discusses such a review in this way:

> The corrections made through this process will enhance the accuracy of the case study, hence increasing the construct validity of the study. In addition, where no objective truth may exist, the procedure

should help to identify the various perspectives, which can then be represented in the case study report.

Maintaining a chain of evidence is important. In order to ensure construct validity and reliability, Yin (1989) recommends that a case study be constructed such that a reader or external observer will be able to trace from the conclusions back to the initial research questions or from the research questions to the conclusions. This concern was addressed by creating a detailed *narrative case study explaining the causal experiences of the participants*.

Internal validity aims to establish causal relationships (Yin, 1994, p 40). With internal validity *"we can infer that a relationship between two variables is causal or that the absence of a relationship implies the absence of cause."* For example, the findings from competence trust were matched with direct economic perceived benefits and technology-performance related risks to see if they correlated. Similarly, the findings from predictability and goodwill trust were matched against relationship-related benefits, strategic benefits, and relational and general risks.

External validity establishes a domain in which the study's findings can be generalized (Yin, 1994, p 41). Another term for external validity is generalizability. Critics typically state that single cases offer a poor basis for generalizability. Case studies are commonly misunderstood for a lack of external validity resulting from not satisfying well-accepted "sampling logic." An accepted rationale for the legitimate use of one critical case to test well-formulated theory exists. However, such criticisms are implicit when contrasting the situation with survey research, where a sample (if selected correctly) is readily generalized to a large universe. This analogy is incorrect when dealing with case studies, because a survey research relies on statistical generalization, whereas case studies (as with experiments) rely on analytical generalization (Yin, 1994, p 43). This study examined multiple cases using the same semi-structured questionnaire (i.e., replication logic). It thereby paved a way for analytical generalizations.

Reliability minimizes errors and biases in the study by demonstrating that the same questionnaire was applied across all cases. The underlying concern of reliability is *"whether the process of the study is consistent, reasonably stable over time, across researchers, and methods"* (Miles and Huberman, 1994, p 278). The multiple case studies took place in a real world setting, and by nature they are highly unlikely to recur and to be observed again in the same way. The following techniques were applied in order to ensure reliability.

- All cases followed the same semi-structured questionnaire and procedures and used a standard interview protocol (the semi-structured questionnaire). Hence, a well-documented case study protocol provided a guide for external reviews to examine the reliability;

- An effort was made to establish an independent case study database which was categorized and organized;

- Multiple participants from different cases were involved during the interview sessions (see Table 18);

- Triangulation of data sources was used;

- Written notes of the interviews and tabular materials were recorded. The central component of the case study database was, however, the case study narrative. This attempted to synthesize different data sources and present a sequence of events that occurred in the organization with some coherence;

- Data analysis followed best practices from previous research applied in this study.

Following Yin's arguments, this study expands and generalizes theories (analytic generalization) using case studies, rather than enumerating frequencies (statistical generalization). It is believed that the generalizability of the tested inter-organizational trust relationships and its impact on e-commerce participation has been strengthened by using replication logic in multiple case studies. Generalizability describes a theory that has been tested. Specified patterns in trading partner relationships have been matched by empirical data using the same patterns across a range of settings in other cases. Table 18 provides the duration and the number of participants including the type of e-commerce applications in the case studies.

Table 18: Time table of the empirical case studies

Time Cycle	Empirical Research Process	Number of participants	Type of E-Commerce Application
Aug 1999-Oct 1999 Multiple-Case Studies	NZ Customs Uni-Directional dyad – 1 Bi-Directional dyad - A	10	EDI/VANs X400, X25 Internet via ISP
Nov 1999 – Jan 2000 Multiple-Case Studies	Electronic Commerce Network (ECN) Internet Service Provider Uni-Directional dyad – 2 Bi-Directional dyad - A	2	X400 X25 Internet
Jan 2000 – Mar 2000 Multiple-Case Studies	Customs Broker Uni-Directional dyad – 3 Bi-Directional dyad - B	2	Trade Manager
Feb 2000– Mar 2000 Multiple-Case Studies	Pak Ltd (Importer) Uni-Directional dyad – 4 Bi-Directional dyad – B	2	Trade Manager
Jan 2000-Mar 2000 Multiple-Case Studies	Cisco NZ Uni-Directional dyad – 5 Bi-Directional dyad – C	10	Extranet – the initiator Cisco Connection Online
Jan 2000-Mar 2000 Multiple-Case Studies	Compaq NZ Uni-Directional dyad – 6 Bi-Directional dyad – C	4	Extranet – respond to Cisco's extranet
Mar 2000–May 2000 Multiple-Case Studies	Siemens NZ Uni-Directional dyad – 7 Bi-Directional dyad – D	4	Extranet – the initiator – Mainstream express
Mar 2000–May 2000 Multiple-Case Studies	Telecom NZ Uni-Directional dyad – 8 Bi-Directional dyad – D	6	Extranet – respond to Siemen's Extranet

INSTRUMENTATION OF THE CONCEPTUAL MODEL

The case study semi-structured questionnaire was designed to test the conceptual model. The following design guidelines were used in the design of the questionnaire.

(1)   Investigating, exploring, and examining qualitative issues relating to the importance of inter-organizational trust in e-commerce participation was

the main concern, since inter-organizational trust was a newly identified phenomenon. Questions were related to how, why, and in what situations.

(2) Questions were closely linked to the constructs, sub-concepts, and dimensions of the conceptual model, thereby focusing on the relevance of this study.

(3) The design of the questionnaire paved the way for open discussions and candid conversations from the participants, in addition to answering the specific questions. The instrumentation of the conceptual model is enclosed in the appendix followed by the case study questionnaire.

DATA ANALYSIS

Pattern matching was used to analyze the findings from the interviews. Data analysis was carried out in the following manner:

- Analyzing the findings;

- Identifying similarities and differences in the opinions of participants from the same organization;

- Identifying similarities and differences between organizations within the same bi-directional dyad;

- Undertaking a cross-case analysis of the findings between inter-organizational dyads. Moreover, the use of likert type scales was employed to elicit respondents' preferences, thereby adding to a qualitative analysis.

Data analysis was conducted using both qualitative explanations in the form of direct quotes, explanations (narrative description), and quantitative analysis (in the form of a likert scale, as in Low (0-3), Medium (4-6), and High (7-10)).

- Case study descriptions were the starting point in examining the organizations' backgrounds. Moreover, the descriptions provided insights into key activities, events, and organizational issues. This paved a way for analyzing the case study and allowed the researcher to develop normative statements within the limitations and constraints of the research design.

*   The analysis focused on revealing themes via pattern matching. Thus, the process underlying the analysis consisted of iterative cycles of data interpretation along with discussion among researchers and participants from e-commerce organizations. After analyzing and elaborating the individual cases, similar patterns and themes were identified across cases for generalizations. According to Yin (1994), a case study analysis involves "examining, categorizing, tabulating or otherwise recombining evidence to invoke the initial propositions of a [case] study." Yin outlines two analytical strategies: relying on theoretical propositions and developing a case description. The latter is useful when theoretical propositions are absent. "Relying on theoretical propositions" is used when the original objectives and design of the case study are based on the research propositions. This, in turn, reflects a set of research questions and/or hypotheses and literature reviews. The research propositions focused attention on analyzing relevant data. This research used "relying on theoretical propositions," thus focusing on the conceptual model of inter-organizational trust in business-to-business e-commerce participation.

Similarities and differences in the opinions and perceptions of participants within the same organization were initially sought. Where there were differences in their opinions within the same uni-directional dyad (organization), further explanations were requested. Scanned data from each participant identified similarities and differences through pattern matching. In addition, background information about the organization's e-commerce applications and adoption process from existing documents was also analyzed. Documents examined included: organizational charts, trading partner agreements, product information from brochures, web sites, security policies, performance assessments, quality standards, and background information. Finally, a cross case analysis was carried out between an inter-organizational dyad (i.e., two organizations). It is in this stage that meaningful analytical generalizations were derived from causal explanations and narrative descriptions.

In this chapter we described the multiple case study research strategy. Furthermore, we justified the choice of a multiple case study research method and described the research process, which included data collection, instrumentation, data analysis, and data reporting procedures. In the next chapter we report and discuss the findings of the multiple case studies.

Chapter V

Findings
and
Discussion

Chapter 4 provided a description and discussion of the research method chosen to test the conceptual model of inter-organizational trust in e-commerce participation. In this chapter, we report and discuss the findings of the bi-directional dyads by first providing the background information of each case followed by their findings based on the research propositions. Finally, we discuss the findings from a cross-case analysis leading to similarities and differences of the findings.

BACKGROUND OF THE UNI-DIRECTIONAL DYADS

Uni-directional Dyad 1: NZ Customs (Bi-directional Dyad A)

NZ Customs is a large public sector organization with 700 employees. NZ Customs undertakes the clearance of importing and exporting documents. NZ Customs uses CusMod (Customs Modernization), a complex and sophisticated alert system to perform intelligence testing using message queue series (a priority-based software). CusMod uses X400 with Electronic-Data-Interchange (EDI) to integrate all information and electronic processes involved in identifying and processing goods and passengers. CusMod is unique because it facilitates trade internationally and undertakes a back-end imaging audit. A copy of the transaction is produced automatically for each adjustment made to a transaction. CusMod business functions include providing clearance service and information regarding import and export of goods, services, and people coming in and leaving the country, both nationally and internationally.

The New Zealand government's investment in implementing CusMod has put NZ Customs in the forefront of innovation worldwide. The objectives of CusMod are as follows:

- to have all invoice information transmitted electronically before shipment;

- to enable pre-clearance of most shipments;

- to enable consistency of declarations to Customs;

- to reduce customs clearance costs through the elimination of line fees; and

- to assist with the automated calculation of landed costs.

The dyad in this case consists of NZ Customs and their ISP. NZ Customs outsource part of their business-to-business e-commerce processes to their Internet Service Provider who facilitates the movement of business transactions between NZ Customs and their trading partners. The business transactions include cargo information, shipping documentation, clearance documents, and passenger information (both flight and sea) transmitted through CusMod. All incoming transactions have to go through the Internet Service Provider before coming into NZ Customs. NZ Customs has more than 200 trading partners that include customs brokers (agents), regular importers, and exporters.

The ISP is a trade facilitator and has no interest in competing with NZ Customs. In this dyad, NZ Customs (trustor) is supposed to trust their service provider (ISP). NZ Customs also interacts directly with the trading partners (exporters and importers).

Uni-directional Dyad 2: Electronic Commerce Network Ltd (Bi-directional Dyad A)

The Internet Service Provider (Electronic Commerce Network Ltd. ECN) provides e-commerce services for NZ Customs and their trading partners (exporters and importers). ECN was established in 1991, and is New Zealand's leading trusted electronic business intermediary. ECN's main role is to facilitate technical and operational processes for organizations that want to adopt business-to-business e-commerce. They provide services that enable business transactions across any network between applications. In addition, the ISP provides other services, such as 24 hours, 7 days a week availability of the network and maintenance of network, help desk, maintenance of trading partners' details (as in correct information and privacy of trading partners' details), fault reporting, and maintaining direct debit authority schedule. The ISP outsourcers their client-based technological services and operations to almost four thousand trading partners. The ISP director commented:

> Sometimes the ISP needs to deliver EDIFACT format types of messages. During these times we will charge the customs broker a transaction fee for receiving and transmitting messages in EDIFACT format. We do consult with other trading partners regarding electronic trading, as most small businesses lack the financial resources, knowledge, skills, and awareness of the full potential of Internet e-commerce applications, and in order to remain competitive in the global e-commerce market, trading partners outsource their business transactions to us.

The dyad in this case is between the Internet Service Provider and NZ Customs. In this dyad the Internet Service Provider (trustor) is supposed to trust NZ Customs.

Uni-directional Dyad 3: Customs Broker (Bi-directional Dyad B)

The dyad in this case is between a customs broker and an importer. The customs broker clears the goods for the importer through NZ Customs. The customs broker provides customs clearance services for importers and exporters and plays the role of a trade facilitator. Although the customs broker has been using the "Trade Manager" software program for the past three years, they have been trading with the importer for the past 10 years.

The customs broker Customs Agent Wellington Limited (CAWL) is a small company consisting of seven employees. Their business reach is local (that is, within the Wellington region, where they serve 15 importers (their trading partners)). They use Trade Manager, a software program designed to meet the needs of New Zealand exporters and importers. Trade Manager is an e-commerce application which uses Microsoft Access with Visual Basic applications, and provides real-time tracking information. Trade Manager is connected to major couriers, postal services, shipping companies, and ports. Exporters use shipping companies with web sites to link their details to the customs broker's web site. Exporters use Trade Manager to prepare export documentation including invoices, shipper letters of instruction, picking and packing lists, order acknowledgments, and certificates of origin and customs declarations. Importers use Trade Manager to manage orders, keep a database of all their shipments, and calculate accurate landed costs. By doing so, trading partners can track their goods through this site, thereby adding value to their export service. In this dyad, the customs broker (trustor) is supposed to trust the importer.

Uni-directional Dyad 4: Importer (Bi-directional Dyad B)

The dyad in this case is between the importer and the customs broker. The importer obtains clearance for its goods through the customs broker. The importer is a small company with thirteen employees. They import kitchen gadgets, plastics, baby wear, and cosmetics, and distribute them to the five largest supermarkets in New Zealand (including Woolworth, New Worlds, Big Fresh, Countdown, and Pak and Save). The importer has been using Trade Manager for the past five years. Their business transactions include invoices, line items, local charges, freight charges, and storage charges. Most of the charges are automatically calculated by Trade Manager via pre-arranged agreement on prices and charges. Thus, when a shipment arrives at the port, the importer provides information to its customs broker who will then process the clearance of its shipment through customs. In this dyad the importer (trustor) is supposed to trust its customs broker.

Uni-directional Dyad 5: Cisco NZ
(Bi-directional Dyad C)

The dyad in this case is between Cisco NZ and Compaq NZ. Cisco supplies computer and data communication products to Compaq, who integrates computer systems for its end customers.

Cisco NZ, established seven years ago, is a small to medium-sized organization with twenty employees located in Wellington, New Zealand. Its reach is international and its product line is data and communication. Cisco had a sales volume of US $480 billion, with 25,000 employees worldwide. Cisco Systems, Inc. is the second largest company in the world after Microsoft.

Cisco NZ joined forces with its head office in San Jose, California (U.S.) to implement its e-commerce applications. Cisco's business-to-business e-commerce extranet application, Cisco Connections Online (CCO), has built-in functions and business transactions such as purchase orders for equipment, delivery, and product information from web sites. Secondary elements include ordering for equipment, delivery, and ability to check lead track time. Cisco's registered trading partners can download product, equipment, and pricing information from CCO. In addition, automated online tools are embedded within the system.

CCO is the foundation of interactive, networked services that provide immediate and open access to Cisco's information, resources, and systems, anytime and anywhere. Figure 6 depicts the functions and processes embedded within CCO. Cisco embraces the Global Networked Business model, which aims to implement innovative tools and systems, and to share information with diverse company stakeholders, such as suppliers, distributors, customers, and employees. By using CCO, Internetworking Product Center (IPC), and Partner Initiated Customer Access (PICA), Cisco is able to connect trading partners to the manufacturing resource planning system (Cisco, 1998).

Most of Cisco's trading partners are system integrators. They include Logical, Datacom, Compaq, IBM, Telecom, Unisys, Clear, Fujistu, and Computer Link. Cisco's trading partners were chosen on the basis of their reputation and by replicability as a channel. Trading partners are contracted for between three and five years to trade with Cisco NZ. In this dyad Cisco NZ (trustor) is supposed to trust Compaq NZ.

Uni-directional Dyad 6: Compaq NZ
(Bi-directional Dyad C)

The dyad in this case is between Compaq and Cisco NZ. Compaq NZ sells computers, application software, hardware, networks, and databases, undertakes systems integration, and develops database application systems. Compaq's main role is to manufacture computer systems integration parts and provide computer services.

Compaq NZ is a large company with 300 employees and its reach is both national and global. The Wellington branch is responsible for implementing business-to-business e-commerce via e-mail and files, but mostly uses CCO (Cisco's extranet application). Compaq manages Cisco's orders relating to system integration, applies network equipment, and directs products and prices to meet end customer needs. Compaq has five branches in New Zealand; one each in Wellington, Auckland, Christchurch, Hamilton, and Dunedin. In this dyad, Compaq NZ (the trustor) is supposed to trust Cisco NZ (trustee).

Uni-directional Dyad 7: Siemens NZ
(Bi-directional Dyad D)

The dyad in this case is between Siemens NZ and Telecom NZ. Siemens NZ supplies telecommunications products to Telecom NZ.

Siemens NZ consists of Siemens Communication Systems, Siemens Nixdorf, and Siemens Building Technologies Ltd. Siemens Information and Communication Networks Group was established in 1997. Siemens NZ is one of the world's leading providers of end-to-end solutions for voice, data, and mobile communication networks. With more than 16 years experience in the New Zealand market, Siemens NZ is firmly established as a leading provider of electrical, electronic, information, and communications technology. Siemens NZ has since learned that success requires relationship marketing, up-to-date designs, and attention to costs. The Information and Communication network group provides products, systems solutions, service, and support for installation and maintenance of complete corporate and service provider networks. Siemens NZ products include keyphone systems, PABX systems, Call Center applications, voicemail, Integrated Cordless phones, Computer Telephone Integration (CTI), Interactive Voice Response, and Video Conferencing equipment. Siemens Information and Communication networks division is a key supplier of broadband network technology to Telecom NZ.

Siemens NZ implemented an extranet e-commerce application called Mainstream Express. This extranet application is an information communication network, which enables electronic transmission of business-to-business e-commerce transactions. Mainstream Express is user-friendly software with an informal structure using a set of menu options to choose from. Mainstream Express provides the latest product information, technical updates, news, and sales tools, fun, and games. In addition, Mainstream Express has customized information and the presence of a web site with ordering and tracking. This dyad is between Siemens NZ (the trustor) who is supposed to trust Telecom NZ.

Uni-directional Dyad 8: Telecom NZ (Bi-directional Dyad D)

The dyad in this case is between Telecom NZ and Siemens NZ. Telecom purchases telecommunication parts from Siemens NZ and manufactures telecommunication products for its end customers. Telecom products include mobile phones, Internet access, Telco service, and all forms of telecommunications, mobile, and Internet services. Telecom is a large international organization, with 500 employees situated in the Wellington branch. The Logistics group and network delivery section of Telecom handles the operation of applications and implementation from the corporate supply group. The Telecom staff log onto Siemens extranet application Mainstream Express in order to obtain product information, place orders, and retrieve real-time tracking information. In this dyad Telecom NZ (the trustor) is supposed to trust Siemens NZ. In the next section, we discuss the findings of the study based on the research propositions.

FINDINGS BY RESEARCH PROPOSITIONS FROM ALL UNI-DIRECTIONAL DYADS

R-P 1: Trading Partner Trust is Positively Associated with the Perceived Benefits of E-Commerce.

Uni-directional-dyad – 1: NZ Customs R-P: 1

The data suggesting the existence of competence, predictability, and goodwill trust leading to increased perceived economic, relationship-related, and strategic benefits of e-commerce was strongly supported by NZ Customs. For example, competence trust was rated high because NZ Customs outsourced part of their customs clearance process to their ISP (Electronic Commerce Network Ltd) who was responsible for training NZ Customs' staff. The NZ Customs' trading partners consist of custom brokers, exporters, and importers who have shown their ability and skills to operate business-to-business e-commerce transactions. NZ Customs' intranet administrator indicated:

> Of course, like any other new system we were trained to use the CusMod. Initially there were errors, as both our staff and trading partners had to learn to use CusMod. Trading partners had to bear the transaction costs if they continued to make errors, as they were required to re-send the same transaction correctly again. In the long run, trading partners realized the additional costs, and made every effort to get it correct. For example, when we first implemented export entries using CusMod, in October 1996, the error rate was 40-50%, but now it has dropped to 10%. This saves us a lot of time on phone calls, and enabled us to focus on other important aspects leading to strategic decisions, thus contributing to economic and strategic benefits.

> Furthermore, CusMod is 90% automated as the authorization and clearance process is conducted automatically. There is about 10% human intervention, which comes from an alert (i.e., in the case of drug use or fraud). Economic benefits experienced by NZ Customs staff include elimination of duplication and reduced delays in approving cleared goods, thus having a more productive workforce with fewer personnel. In addition, better intelligence systems allowed risks to be more readily and accurately identified. CusMod saved operating costs while improving service, as well as introducing common tariff classifications that enabled shipment of cargoes to and from international markets. This, in turn, benefits importers and exporters who received clearance electronically, as they need not pay for couriers, and no paper was involved thus contributing to importers and exporters economic benefits.

The findings showed that standardized, structured routine procedures involved in customs clearance contributed to economic benefits from consistent competence and predictability trust, leading to savings in costs. Further, NZ Customs was able to eliminate paper, as there was no need to store backups (no offsite storage). In the past, records for almost seven million transactions had to be stored, and the costs of storing several tons of paper led to maintenance problems.

Consistent behaviours in the ISP's interactions and its ability to transact in the customs documents in the required format enabled NZ Customs to predict its ISP's actions contributing to relational benefits. The ISP kept its business promises and adhered to policies, contract terms, and trading partner agreements.

Relationship-related benefits experienced by NZ Customs include:

• Improved communication and cooperation with their ISP;

• Information sharing (that is accurate, timely, speedy, complete, and relevant); and

• Increased level of commitment with their trading partners.

NZ Customs also experienced goodwill trust. Although NZ Customs did provide initial support to their importers and exporters in business-to-business operations, it can be a complex area for new trading partners. Hence, trading partners' willingness to share information and provide support relating to e-commerce adoption was rated medium for goodwill trust, and an NZ Customs consultant indicated:

> We work as a team and perceive benefits as a win-win situation. Positive feelings towards our trading partners is high, because NZ Customs played an influential role in information sharing because of our strong international networks and reputation for ethical behaviour, efficiency, effectiveness, and innovation.

The ISP was willing to share information and did provide support, thus building goodwill trust. Furthermore, importers and exporters did demonstrate care and concern in important decisions. The findings implied that trading partner trust played not only an important role in business-to-business e-commerce operations in NZ Customs who represented the nation, but also contributed to economic, relationship-related, and strategic benefits.

Uni-directional-dyad – 2: ISP R-P: 1

The data suggesting the existence of competence, predictability, and goodwill trust leading to increased perceived economic, relationship-related, and strategic benefits of e-commerce was supported by the ISP. The ISP director stated:

> We believe that trust is important since our trading partners are the ones who actually input the data into the system for responses. Therefore, training our trading partners to use e-commerce applications correctly is important. We experienced relationship-related benefits from open communications and satisfaction of NZ Customs staff.

The ISP had regular face-to-face meeting with NZ Customs staff. The findings implied that trading partner relationship and trust is the key to sustained e-commerce participation, and it fosters open communications, information sharing, and tolerance for mistakes.

Uni-directional-dyad – 3: Customs Broker R-P: 1

The data suggesting the existence of competence, predictability, and goodwill trust leading to increased perceived economic, relationship-related, and strategic benefits of e-commerce was strongly supported by the customs broker. The customs broker rated competence trust to be high, because Trade Manager application was a simple, user-friendly application. The customs broker noted:

> We experienced economic benefits from a major reduction of paper flow, automatic storage of information through computer backup procedures, direct clearance cost savings, reduction of clerical work, and reduction by one day in transit time.

The automated clearance process involved in customs clearance may lead to fewer errors, and transactions are cleared more quickly, thus contributing to economic benefits from savings in time and cost. Economic benefits such as non-duplication of efforts, immediate access to data without disruption to workflow, greater accuracy with fewer input functions, and timely output of tracking information has enabled better utilization of human resources.

Economic benefits led to relationship-related benefits because the provision of timely, accurate, complete, and correct information contributed to satisfaction of the importer. The customs broker indicated that relationship-related benefits came from cooperation.

> We cooperate and communicate openly, as we use the same application. We also pay indemnity insurance for the importer's paper work (as a way of sharing risks).

Relationship-related benefits were derived from the trading partner trust relationships that were built over the years before the company began using Trade Manager. We define trust as being reliable, credible, and honest in a business relationship, and honoring the quality of information. The findings implied that long-term trading partner relationships established with the importer contributed to relationship-related benefits.

Uni-directional-dyad – 4: Importer R-P: 1

The data suggesting the existence of competence, predictability, and goodwill trust leading to increased perceived economic, relationship-related, and strategic benefits of e-commerce was strongly supported by the importer. Competence trust was rated high because the importer found Trade Manager to be user-friendly software. The importer asserted that:

> Our customs broker responded to our queries through e-mail, telephone, fax, and in getting the freight charges loaded into the system within a couple of hours (that is less than half a day), thus contributing to economic benefits from savings in time and costs. Economic benefits from savings in time and cost from making telephone calls or waiting for the information was experienced as the Trade Manager provided real-time tracking information. We were aware when the goods will be cleared and were better able to inform our suppliers. Furthermore, we only had to bring in our delivery order, which was electronically sent into our system by the customs broker. It takes less than twenty minutes to clear.

Relationship-related benefits were seen from open communications and information sharing. In the words of the importer:

The customs broker has shown a willingness to share information, and provided support when we first implemented Trade Manager. The customs broker's staff came over and gave us some training. They did show care and concern not only in using the technology, but also in making important strategic decisions, such as designing a cost-effective approach for shipping and transport.

The importer went on to say:

Although we had a choice to do business with other customs brokers, we preferred to trade with our customs broker because of past experiences that contributed to a foundation of familiarity. We have been trading with them for almost ten years.

The findings implied that trading partner trust was high in this dyad. Embedded automated protocols in the Trade Manager provided technical efficiencies, and together with competence trust in Trade Manager, economic benefits leading to enhanced trading partner trust were experienced. Satisfaction from real-time tracking information of the clearance process increased the importer's trust with its suppliers and contributed to relationship-related benefits.

Uni-directional-dyad – 5: Cisco NZ R-P: 1
The data suggesting that the existence of competence, predictability, and goodwill trust leading to increased perceived economic, relationship-related, and strategic benefits of e-commerce was not strongly supported by Cisco. Cisco rated competence trust of Compaq NZ to be low. One possible explanation for this is that although their extranet application Cisco Connection Online (CCO) is a user-friendly package, the process involved in creating an order for the products and components is a complex one. CCO undertakes an automated checking mechanism, thereby contributing to 80% of the fault activities reported on the Web. Cisco's accounting manager commented:

We have some trading partners who can perform competently, and some that cannot but have learnt it the painful way in terms of wasted time and costs, as they need to re-send the same order twice. Some of our trading partners do not have the underlying fundamental knowledge to place complete and correct orders, thereby, lacking the intellectual horsepower required to undertake the ordering process.

The online ordering process permits Compaq staff to check the pricing and configuration of the order even before placing the actual order. Improved order accuracy from the interactive web-based applications (with built-in rules and access to current pricing, product specifications, and selection/configurations) ensured the submission of complete and accurate orders. Through CCO, Compaq staff was able to learn about Cisco's products and pricing, create an order, download software updates, search for known bugs, and resolve technical problems through the state-of-the-art network technical assistance applications.

In fact, 80% of the non-technical support questions were answered online through Cisco's convenient, self-service applications that in turn increased Compaq's satisfaction. Compaq received immediate, round-the-clock access to richer, more precise service and support information, thus contributing to economic and relationship-related benefits.

Relationship-related benefits further help to improve communication and cooperation with Compaq staff through constant e-mails and phone calls made to the Cisco's IT call center in Sydney – the Internet Business Solutions Group (IBSG). The IBSG provided additional clarifications to the technical jargon, product information to check if Cisco's trading partners were using the system properly, and other communication involved in the process. Compaq staff will need to be aware of the right parts, and are therefore dependent on Cisco for their actual products (which include data and communication equipment, technical advice, and support to place an order). A Cisco Sales Consultant indicated that:

> Compaq staff is aware of the market coverage and is confident in their capability in resolving standardized issues. Over time Compaq staff have shown an ability to be competent channel system integrators using Cisco computer and communication equipment.

Consistent behaviours from Compaq staff in their ability to use CCO correctly gave an indication of their performance capability and confidence, and therefore increased their predictability trust. Compaq was thus able to fulfill end customers' preference, and experience relationship-related benefits. Compaq staff was willing to share information regarding the amount of stock they required for an advanced period of time. A Cisco sales consultant indicated that Compaq staff was aware that Cisco is popular and had a reputation. Hence, by undertaking e-business with Cisco, Compaq's reputation has also improved.

Cisco provided Compaq staff with initial training that was found encouraging and supportive, as they were willing to share information relating to e-commerce adoption. Cisco NZ has a brand name and an increased level of technical knowledge, which enhanced Compaq's reputation. The findings implied that Cisco's powerful tool, CCO, has embedded automated protocols that provided reliable and timely information for Compaq staff, who experienced both economic and relationship-related benefits.

Uni-directional-dyad – 6: Compaq NZ R-P: 1

The data suggesting the existence of competence, predictability, and goodwill trust leading to increased perceived economic, relationship-related, and strategic benefits of e-commerce was strongly supported by Compaq NZ. For example, Cisco's configuration tool enabled Compaq staff to configure their orders. A Compaq network sales specialist described how:

> CCO enables us to check the prices, request a discount if necessary, and electronically receive an estimated time of arrival before even confirming the order. The system automatically gives the number of days as to when the goods will be delivered, thereby enabling Compaq staff to undertake an inquiry on the system in advance. The updated information on Cisco's website is accurate and reliable. Cisco kept their business promises which assisted Compaq to make better strategic decisions, thus contributing to economic benefits from savings in time and costs (from telephone calls).

> Competence trust was shown by Cisco staff who had the ability to do their job. Cisco staff is the 'pros' as they know what they are doing. Their IT support people are excellent, very responsive, and timely in providing complete and accurate information. In addition, their online tools have checking mechanisms that enabled Compaq to detect errors. Compaq staff are able to say that trading with Cisco is better than trading with most of Cisco's competitors, particularly when it comes to problem-solving which creates a confidence in handling conflict resolution and clarifying issues. I guess that's why

Cisco is number two in the world and it is definitely based on reputation and goodwill trust. – Compaq Network Specialist Manager.

Compaq staff observed economic benefits from reduced operations, transaction and administrative costs due to quick responses and timely, accurate information retrieved from Cisco's extranet application. A Compaq network sales specialist manager described their benefits as:

We have experienced reduced error rates and improved accuracy of information exchanged, as we can configure our orders and check them first before confirming the placement of the same order. Faster responses to orders and reduced lead time from CCO provided estimated arrival dates of the goods and tracking information which enabled us to inform our end consumers.

Hence, Compaq NZ experienced reduced inventory levels and optimized their supply chain because there was no need to keep stock. The stock arrives, is cleared at Customs, and then gets delivered directly to the end customers. The Compaq NZ Network Sales Specialist indicated that they were dependent on Cisco staff.

Cisco's staff are reliable. We want to continue using Cisco's communication equipment for two reasons. First, Compaq NZ's end customers rely on Compaq as system integrators, and second, Compaq end customers order Cisco's equipment, which only Cisco can supply. In that respect Compaq was dependent on Cisco.

Most of Compaq's end customers require Cisco products and equipment because of Cisco's brand name and reputation. Although Compaq has been using CCO for the past eighteen months, Compaq had a trading partner relationship with Cisco for the previous ten years. Cisco NZ has a big commitment to make things work. Cisco's staff does back-end work to constantly check all incoming orders in order to make sure that the orders sent are complete and correct. Cisco staff have shown consistent behaviours in their business interactions with Compaq staff. Although the focus may point towards a high level of competent trust in technology and financial resources, soft relationships (such as honesty in providing reliable information and having a call centre when problems arise) were found to be important. The availability of financial resources can purchase any fancy e-commerce tool, but the key is not only in having the right skilled staff to manage the technology but also in having committed trading partners.

The increased level of commitment from Cisco NZ led to long term contracts that lasted between three and five years. Building trust and trading partner relationships was important because Cisco NZ was aware of the products. Compaq participants indicated that they trusted Cisco staff. Trust matters in e-commerce trading partner relationships, although it is implicit. As one Compaq NZ Network specialist commented:

> We speak of trust in e-commerce systems with regard to actual dealings, but it takes some time for trading partner relationship trust to gradually develop.

The findings implied that the technological efficiencies of CCO initially contributed to economic benefits for Compaq that in turn led to satisfaction and relationship-related benefits.

Uni-directional-dyad – 7: Siemens NZ R-P: 1

The data suggesting the existence of competence, predictability, and goodwill trust leading to increased perceived economic, indirect, relationship-related, and strategic benefits of e-commerce was strongly supported by Siemens NZ. Siemens staff rated competence trust of Telecom staff to be medium. The Siemens Customer Marketing Manager described:

> Although Telecom staff have the competence, they continued to send us incomplete purchase orders with errors. We had to provide support and training to Telecom staff all the time.

> Each time an order came in we checked and verified the order manually. If the order came in incomplete, it will not do the job so we informed Telecom NZ using e-mail that we cannot accept the order and explaining the reasons. We educate them, so that their customers will have confidence in them. We even go with their sales team to their clients and explain the system. We do give seminar presentations relating to the functionality and add value of the products we

supply. We write an e-mail news service, which Telecom obtains three times a week, in addition to our newsletters.

Siemens staff experienced economic benefits from reduced administrative work and experienced perceived benefits from improved customer service and product quality. The orders were verified before confirmation, as one Siemens Accounting manager commented:

> Our trading relationships with Telecom have been going on for the last 15 years, although we have been using Mainstream Express for the past three years.

Relationship-related benefits were rated high because of the supplier-customer relationship culture that Siemens practiced. Siemens participants indicated that they involved a lot of risk-taking from the supplier's perspective. Buyers only looked for trading partners that were easy to do business with and when a problem arose, Siemens NZ were expected to be quick, reliable, and efficient in fixing the problem. A Siemens NZ networking manager stated:

> Telecom staff often provided us with forecast information that enabled better planning so that we can supply the orders in a timely manner. We maintained a regular buffer stock in case of urgent demands. 90% of the time the orders that came in were correct. The fault in the remaining 10% was due to items that were complex and required additional technical knowledge.

A Siemens NZ accounting manager indicated that:

> There were fewer telephone calls and e-mails, as they stopped calling us. Positive feelings sometimes depend on who you are speaking to, and can be a perception, which can change from one event to another. Telecom staff was willing to put in the effort and invest in their trading partner relationships, thus developing goodwill trust.

> We are known for having up-to-date products as 50% of our products are less than eighteen months old. This is not a reciprocal arrangement. Our reputation is based on our solutions that assist

Telecom customers to maintain their competitive advantage in an increasingly challenging environment thus contributing to strategic benefits. Having a contract means nothing because it only spells out the procedures and does not mean that an order will come in. Sometimes we move at a cost minus (loss) situation, and we feel whether it is worth while doing the business.

The findings implied that Siemens NZ made every effort to build and maintain its trading partner relationship and trust with Telecom NZ.

Uni-directional-dyad – 8: Telecom NZ R-P: 1

The data suggesting the existence of competence, predictability, and goodwill trust leading to increased perceived economic, relationship-related, and strategic benefits of e-commerce was supported by Telecom staff. Telecom staff rated competence trust of Siemens NZ to be high. A Telecom NZ accounting manager commented:

Siemens NZ staff was competent and reliable, and they do provide us with adequate operational support in the form of training.

Timely and reliable information contributed to economic benefits, and fewer telephone calls and e-mails. Furthermore, information sharing takes place when there is an early identification of problems. Siemens staff found ways to solve problems within a reasonable time scale that fit the needs and operations, thus contributing to satisfaction and relationship-related benefits. A Telecom NZ accounting manager indicated:

Siemens NZ had access to our forecasting information, business development, and we know what price we have been charged for their products, as it was pre-arranged in the contract. There were signs of improved communication and cooperation with Siemens staff as they shared information that was accurate, timely, fast, complete, and relevant. According to the Telecom NZ Transport Manager, we were able to receive accurate tracking information of the goods we ordered.

Goodwill trust and strategic benefits were not supported by Telecom NZ due to a high turnover of Telecom staff. The findings implied that there was a gradual increase in the benefits derived from trading partner trust.

R-P 2: Trading Partner Trust is Negatively Associated with Perceived Risks of E-Commerce.

Uni-directional-dyad – 1: NZ Customs R-P: 2

The data suggesting the existence of competence, predictability, and goodwill trust leading to decrease in the perceived technology performance-related, relational, and general risks of e-commerce was strongly supported by NZ Customs. For example, NZ Customs rated technology performance-related risks to be low to begin with because their ISP was responsible for the compatibility and security of e-commerce applications. The NZ Customs intranet administrator commented:

> The ISP was responsible for the compatibility of the system among the trading partners (importers and exporters) and the CusMod system. Hence, compatibility of the system was not an issue because the ISP facilitated the movement of transactions between NZ Customs and their trading partners.

Although the ISP facilitated the technological needs for customs clearance, a few trading partners experienced relational risks. For example, the NZ Customs intranet administrator indicated:

> The development of CusMod and changes associated with business processes and the introduction of the Internet have left some companies reluctant to change and others hampering on our door demanding change, thus contributing to relational risks. We are aware of the culture shock and are trying to be patient with them. Some of our trading partners are loud, hostile, and even aggressive (i.e., related to functional conflict). For example, the Inland Revenue Department (IRD) wanted a list of all our employees and their income to be submitted through a secure web site. The IRD demonstrated absolute power and authority and we had no choice to exercise either politically or financially. We are trying to build partnerships, and while some trading partners are great at demonstrating change, most of them are not.

Like any change, NZ Customs experienced relational risks in the form of coercive power from senior authorities, reluctance to change, and organizational inertia from their trading partners (importers and exporters).

NZ Customs rated perceived general risks from poor business practices to be low. The participants indicated that the customs clearance process was a legislative one and matters can go up to the ministry level. For example, fines and imprisonment can be imposed on the customs broker or importers and exporters who undertake illegal trading practices such as dealing with drugs. The findings emphasized that perceived risks of e-commerce were insignificant on one hand because trading partner trust played an important role, and on the other hand the customs clearance process was a legal one. The ISP indicated that research proposition 2 did not apply to them.

Uni-directional-dyad – 3: Customs Broker R-P: 2
The data suggesting the existence of competence, predictability, and goodwill trust leading to decreased perceived technology performance-related, relational, and general risks of e-commerce was not strongly supported by the customs broker. For example, the customs broker rated technology performance-related risks to be low. One possible explanation for this is that Trade Manager is not a complex web-based application. The customs broker commented:

> Issues arising from the compatibility and infrastructure were few because the Trade Manager was a Microsoft application. In addition, we relied on other forms of communication, such as the fax, telephone, and e-mail. Technology only enables the transmission of data from point to point. We need to trust the person keying in the data that the information is correct. Competence trust enables tracking of accurate information from using Trade Manager by the importer. The Trade Manager enables us to lock our trading partners. All events are recorded against each job, order on a date/time basis, and memos are created and referenced/filed to each job for future reference, thereby enabling importers to achieve lower clearance costs, and creating integrity of the business transactions.

The findings implied that Trade Manager had embedded protocols that detected errors, thus reducing risks.

Uni-directional-dyad – 4: Importer R-P: 2
The data suggesting that the existence of competence, predictability, and goodwill trust leading to decreased perceived technology performance-re-

lated, relational, and general risks of e-commerce was not supported by the importer. The importer rated technology performance-related risks to be medium because the importer suspects that the customs broker exercises poor business practices.

Relational risks arising from uncertainties were rated medium. The importer commented:

> We did face initial uncertainties in using the Trade Manager that led to our dependence on our customs broker. These interdependencies gradually led to an imbalance of power. Although our customs broker provided us with free software and initial training, we were left in a difficult position. It is not something that you have to outsource, but we had to change our internal business processes in order to facilitate and simplify the business processes of the customs broker, which takes some time to get it completely right. We do face situations of conflict and handling discrepancies, but it is more a functional conflict relating to business processes rather than a personal conflict.

Opportunistic behaviours (such as increasing the charges for the goods cleared by the customs broker) were seen as relational risks. According to the importer:

> Our customs broker did appear to exercise opportunistic behaviors by increasing the charges and costs for clearance, which led to functional conflicts derived from a misunderstanding in calculating charges, due to the conversion of currencies, and taxes. In most cases the customs broker had to explain to us on how they derived the figures.

The findings implied that perceived risks were resolved by communicating openly with the customs broker who was willing to explain the situation, thus increasing trading partner trust.

Uni-directional-dyad – 5: Cisco R-P: 2

The data suggesting the existence of competence, predictability, and goodwill trust leading to decreased perceived technology performance-related, relational, and general risks of e-commerce was not strongly supported by Cisco. Technology performance-related risks were rated low because CCO was only implemented by Cisco, and Compaq staff only had to log onto the web site using authorization mechanisms. Relational risks were rated low because although trading partners in a situation of conflict and handling discrepancy do sometimes exhibit frustration or resentment, these issues are business-related and not personal. Cisco's accounting manager commented:

> Conflicts do occur always as nobody wants to kill each other. Occasionally, they do get frustrated when they want something to be done. They negotiate and with cohesion depending on how important the situation is.

Cisco tries to match their objectives with Compaq's goals and occasionally there are cases of differences. Cisco's NZ Accounting manager noted:

> Although, the extranet site was maintained by Cisco it is was fairly secure. There were concerns that Compaq staff could leak out sensitive information (such as price and product information) to Cisco's competitors.

General risks were rated low because Cisco made sure that best business practices in the form of regular audit, high quality standards, checking mechanisms, risk management, and top management support were implemented.

Uni-directional-dyad – 6: Compaq NZ R-P: 2

The data suggesting the existence of competence, predictability, and goodwill trust leading to decreased perceived technology performance-related, relational, and general risks of e-commerce was not strongly supported by Compaq NZ. Technology performance-related risks were rated medium because of Compaq's initial experience in learning how to use the CCO application. Since it is new, it was difficult, but with training and calls made to their help desk, it was possible over time to see the pattern involved in using the CCO application.

Relational risks were rated low by Compaq staff. Compaq participants indicated:

> Cisco staff did create a situation of imbalance of power, as they would like to have the names of our end customers. But when we

chose not to give to them because we would like to have a bit of competition by buying from other suppliers, Cisco staff did not like it.

This was a situation of power exhibited by Cisco that contributed to relational risks. Compaq participants did indicate that Cisco staff could sometimes be arrogant, thus contributing to relational risks.

Uni-directional-dyad – 7: Siemens NZ R-P: 2

The data suggesting the existence of competence, predictability, and goodwill trust leading to decreased perceived technology performance-related, relational, and general risks of e-commerce was not supported by Siemens. Technology performance-related risks were rated low by Telecom because Siemens implemented the extranet application and outsourced it onto a private server. Thus compatibility and security concerns were minimal. Relational risks were rated low. Telecom staff was initially unhappy when Siemens staff accessed their forecast information but later they permitted Siemens staff to access forecast information. Telecom was aware of the stock they required in order to meet incoming demands. Siemens Key accounting manager commented:

> There was an incident when we received a phone call from a Telecom staff for an order and was told that it was an urgent order. We placed the order and when the goods arrived the senior manager asked me why we supplied it. We told that we had received an e-mail and a phone call for this order and the person who made the order said that we misunderstood them and denied placing the order.

For example, Siemens rated predictability trust of Telecom staff to be low because of a lack of consistent behaviours. A Siemens Network manager commented:

> Sometimes we develop trust and goodwill with certain key people in Telecom and the next thing you know they have left the company.

Thus, the high turnover of Telecom staff made it difficult for Siemens to develop stable relationships, and this contributed to relational risks derived from uncertainties and a lack of knowledge. Siemens customer service manager indicated that:

> Everything was a bargain, and sometimes we did not feel confident. Telecom staff kept insisting on reducing the prices. All they wanted was the best price up front, and if we gave them the best deal, then they want another 10% off and if we refused it, we have become difficult to deal with. This has happened two to three times.

> We received the fax and confirmed the order using fax or e-mail that the order has been received. We have to deal with several different people at different levels, especially the people at operational level who do not see the big picture. People at the top level can see the whole picture but do not see the problem hence at times communication becomes challenging and it is to do with the buyer versus seller's culture.

Hence, it was seen that there was a lack of trust (as in open, honest, reliable communication) due to the high turnover of Telecom staff, as Siemens staff had to deal with a different person in Telecom each time. Despite the fact that Siemens NZ gave their best price and service, trading partner relationships and trust were difficult to achieve.

Telecom staff indicated that their end customers were unaware as to where the parts came from, as long as their products operated properly. Siemens' staff interpreted this as not totally true especially at this time, where brand name counts. It is very important to build trading partner trust relationships. The findings implied that Siemens' experience with Telecom staff was open and honest most of the time, although there were incidents of dishonesty which contributed to relational risks.

Uni-directional-dyad – 8: Telecom NZ RP- 2

The data suggesting the existence of competence, predictability, and goodwill trust leading to decreased perceived technology performance-related, relational, and general risks of e-commerce was not supported by Telecom. Technology performance-related risks were rated low because Telecom staff had to log on to a private server. There were concerns in relational risks within Telecom. A Telecom NZ accounting manager indicated:

Our top management commitment was low. Committing to certain important decisions was difficult.

Relational risks were rated medium because of the high turnover of staff, as Siemens had to re-train each new Telecom staff member on how to place orders correctly and completely. This led to relational risks. General risks did not impact Telecom because the system was not connected to Telecom NZ. The findings implied that both technology and trading partner trust played an important role in reducing the risks of e-commerce.

R-P 3: Technology Trust Mechanisms in E-Commerce are Positively Associated with Perceived Benefits of E-Commerce.

Uni-directional-dyad – 1: NZ Customs R-P: 3

The data suggesting the existence of technology trust mechanisms in e-commerce leading to increased perceived economic, relationship-related, and strategic benefits of e-commerce was strongly supported by NZ Customs. NZ Customs rated most of their technology trust mechanisms to be high because the CusMod system was a sophisticated system with embedded automated checking mechanisms and protocols that enabled detection of errors. Furthermore, the ISP provided the technical expertise, training, and support in addition to compatible systems that help build trust.

CusMod is a semi-manual automated system which operates on a round-the-clock basis and demands competence trust from NZ Customs trading partners. CusMod relies on a set of structured messages that run in a sequential number order. The set has to be submitted in a structured format; otherwise the system will reject the transaction. CusMod produces three outputs: namely, CUSDER for customs declaration, CUSCAR for customs cargo, and CURRES for customs response which either confirms or rejects CUSDER and CUSCAR. If the output is confirmed by the system then the system automatically issues a delivery order and an invoice. Otherwise, it returns an error message in the case of insufficient information. NZ Customs' security analyst indicated that the CusMod demands standardized, structured, routine processes. An NZ Customs security analyst indicated:

The CusMod system operates round the clock 24 hours x 7. When NZ Customs first implemented CusMod, they had to face a forty-eight hour turnaround time for clearance, but now it is just under twenty minutes.

It can be seen that with embedded technology trust mechanisms in e-commerce applications, speed and accuracy of business-to-business e-commerce transactions are achieved. The flexibility that CusMod provides (i.e., round-the-clock access) increased the satisfaction of importers and exporters. Consequently, relationship-related benefits were rated high because of the provision of timely, accurate, complete, and correct information. A slight delay in the transactions from CusMod can affect the trust of importers and exporters. Furthermore, NZ Customs receives managerial support from the government. The following mechanisms help to ensure integrity of business transactions and they include:

- Business problems are handled by the NZ Customs call center in Auckland for NZ Customs' trading partners. Importers and exporters can rely on these services if they have any uncertainties;

- Datacom played the role as the NZ Customs' service help desk; and

- The ISP dealt with client-related problems. In addition, NZ Customs worked with the Ministry of Agriculture and Forestry and the Immigration department, thus maintaining high levels of security.

According to the NZ Customs' security analyst:

There is a lot of confidential information in NZ Customs' databases and there is a need to ensure privacy of the information. NZ Customs has installed anti-virus software programs in their computer systems in order to protect the databases. They undertake a daily backup of their system, and practice segregation of duties using swipe cards where certain staffs are forbidden from entering certain floors in the building.

We have a formal code of conduct supported by guidelines on principles, conventions and practices issued by the State Services Commission. We have to set a good example to the public in order to ensure business continuity. We believe that top management commitment is necessary as a business driver in the technology edge. We have to provide a statutory declaration using electronic signatures stating that the goods are cleared.

In addition, NZ Customs experienced best business practices in the following ways. NZ Customs and their trading partners had to abide by the Customs Act. Privacy of information was important. NZ Customs security analyst indicated that each trading partner was allocated a unique identifier (reference ID), which informed NZ Customs that it was an authentic, authorized trading partner. Security audits alerted NZ Customs to implement adequate and complete risk management strategies (such as intelligent system checks). Thus, economic benefits from regular audits provided timely, accurate information.

The findings implied that cooperation among the trading partners (importers and exporters) and the ISP assisted in maintaining security by detecting smuggling offences, protecting flora and fauna, monitoring the movement of strategic (military) goods, investigating revenue fraud, and seizing illegal drugs.

Uni-directional-dyad – 2: ISP R-P: 3

The data suggesting the existence of technology trust mechanisms in e-commerce leading to perceived economic, relationship-related, and strategic benefits of e-commerce was strongly supported by ISP. The ISP director observed:

> Through mapping and translation services, our technology provisions are designed to meet the needs of our trading partners' business requirements, thus creating a gateway for business electronic transactions (including purchase orders, invoices, waybills, compliance with government agencies, and value added services, including payment and fulfillment transactions).

> We do have a firewall in our systems that separate the flow of transactions between our trading partners and the outside public. We allocate unique identifiers for each of our 4,000 trading partners.

The ISP was responsible for implementing e-commerce protocols that provide trust and security-based mechanisms such as confidentiality, integrity, and authentication of business transactions sent by both trading partners.

Trading partners had to log on to the ISP system using User Id's and passwords, thereby achieving transaction integrity, confidentiality, and authentication of the trading partners and the messages. Although technology provided the speed, automation that contributes to economic benefits, relationship-related, and strategic benefits could only be derived in trustworthy trading partner relationships over a period of time where positive consistent behaviours of trading partners were experienced.

The findings implied that the main role of the ISP is to provide technical services for the trading partners based on their business requirements. Importers, exporters, and NZ Customs were able to reap economic benefits from using automated ways of trading. The remaining research propositions did not impact the ISP relationship with NZ Customs, as the ISP was a service provider and was not directly competing with NZ Customs.

Uni-directional-dyad – 3: Customs Broker R-P: 3

The data suggesting the existence of technology trust mechanisms in e-commerce leading to increased perceived economic, relationship-related, and strategic benefits of e-commerce was supported by the customs broker. For example, the customs broker rated most of its trust and security-based mechanisms to be high. Mechanisms such as firewalls and encryption (for confidentiality), digital signatures (for non-repudiation), and network access controls were not implemented by the customs broker because the Trade Manager was a simple Windows Microsoft Access and Visual Basic application system. The customs broker noted that:

> Confirmations' and acknowledgments were received using the e-mail embedded in the Trade Manager. In case of urgent orders we use the telephone, e-mail, or fax.

The findings implied that confidentiality of business-to-business transactions sent and received by the customs broker was not an issue, because the system was not connected to their network. Separate log-on procedures using User Id's and passwords to send and retrieve information were applied. The security issues were limited, as the Trade Manager was a pre-programmed application.

Uni-directional-dyad – 4: Importer R-P: 3

The data suggesting the existence of technology trust mechanisms leading to increased perceived economic, relationship-related, and strategic benefits of e-commerce was strongly supported by the importer. The importer indicated that:

> We used separate log-on procedures and applied segregation of duties in order to ensure different levels of authorization mechanisms in the importer's organization. The receptionist, administration staff, and drivers do not have access to the Trade Manager. Furthermore, we exercised best business practices in the form of daily backups and followed the Importers Institute standard. We maintained a backup hardcopy version of all purchase order numbers, invoice numbers, reference numbers.

Economic benefits in the form of less paper usage and lower error rates were achieved, as a copy of the original invoice was given to the customs broker. They also experienced cheaper flat rates for custom clearance charges (no line fees) including landed cost reports, electronic proof of delivery, reconciliation of deferred payment, and tariff consultancy. The importer noted:

> We had more time (from less administrative work) from automated customs clearance service that enabled us to focus on our strategic planning.

The findings implied that real-time tracking information provided accurate information for the importer to act upon, which contributed to trading partner satisfaction and relationship-related benefits.

Uni-directional-dyad – 5: Cisco NZ R-P: 3
The data suggesting the existence of technology trust mechanisms leading to increased perceived economic, relationship-related, and strategic benefits of e-commerce was strongly supported by Cisco. CCO provides direct access to the manufacturing systems so that Compaq staff can track inventories, engineering changes, shipment status, and other information in real time. Furthermore, Cisco NZ has help desk and system technicians who provide support. The IT customer service in Sydney (ISBG) undertakes to answer queries and offer a second level of service and IT support. Cisco's accounting manager indicated that:

> Initially, the error rate was 80%, has now reduced to less than 15%, thus contributing to economic benefits from savings in time and cost

(telephone calls, e-mail, faxes for correcting mistakes). CCO provides benefits in the form of real-time order tracking information, and estimated arrival dates of goods. In fact, Cisco participants admitted that 35-40% of the revenue came from Compaq NZ.

Economic benefits over a period of time led to positive, consistent behaviors shown by Compaq's improved customer service, product quality, and satisfaction. Cisco saved up to US$800 million dollars per year, as there was no need to re-key the same order information that was entered by our Compaq staff. The provision of real-time online tracking information has contributed to additional savings in time and costs previously handled via telephone calls and fax.

Furthermore, regular system integrity tests and audits were conducted to detect flaws and security concerns in the e-commerce system. Each transaction that came from Cisco's system has a trading partner reference code (as in sequence numbers) together with an order number. Each time an order came in, the system checked and triggered an e-mail back to the trading partner to confirm the receipt of the order. However, if the order was configured wrongly, the system would automatically trigger an error message back to the sender. The Cisco NZ's accounting manager noted:

> We try to resolve issues within twenty-four hours via telephone calls, e-mail and sometimes even face-to-face meetings as Compaq NZ was also located in the Wellington region, thus contributing to relationship-related benefits. Cisco has explicit trading and procedures agreement with Compaq regarding their roles and responsibilities outlined in the System Integration Supply Contract.

He went on to say,

> Compaq staff do adhere to policies, terms of contract, and trading partner agreement. We do sign a three-to five-year contract with our trading partners,' that outline the procedure to be followed from the time we place an order until settlement.

Cisco considers best business practices as the quality and correctness of the information ordered from the services they provide. The incoming orders undergo multiple checks through system security services (confidentiality, privacy, integrity, authenticity, and non-repudiation).

The findings implied that CCO plays an important role in building trading partner trust. Satisfaction derived from technological efficiency laid the groundwork for a trusting relationship to develop between trading partners.

Uni-directional-dyad – 6: Compaq NZ R-P: 3

The data suggesting the existence of technology trust mechanisms in e-commerce leading to increased perceived economic, relationship-related, and strategic benefits of e-commerce was strongly supported by Compaq. The online tracking of information was made available from the time an order was placed until the goods were delivered. Cisco's diagnosis software analyzes and reports software and hardware failures, which includes automatic logging of calls to the Customer Support Center. Compaq participants indicated that:

> Indeed, CCO assisted us in making accurate strategic decisions and building our reputation, as we were able to fulfill our business promises, thus contributing to both economic and relationship-related benefits.

This cyclic process, in turn, built Cisco's reputation as Compaq's end customers continued to order Cisco products.

Other technology trust mechanisms practiced by Compaq staff include authentication mechanisms using User ID's and passwords, application controls, and accounting controls providing reference numbers for the transactions, and the implementation of best business practices. In the words of the Compaq accounting manager:

> We have reference numbers with Cisco NZ that served as unique identifiers thereby providing authentication. We believe that top management commitment is critical especially when it comes to the budget. We do have to meet with the standards set out by Cisco (industry and universal) and policies. We are part of the ISO 9000, but not all of the divisions. We have a trading partner agreement, and undertake regular audit checks in order to manage risks. We have a business risk management group of consultants who design contingency procedures for our e-commerce systems and operations.

The findings implied that Compaq NZ was also applying best business practices in their organization, which made it easier to work and to meet Cisco's high expectations and standards.

Uni-directional-dyad-7: Siemens NZ R-P: 3

The data suggesting the existence of technology trust mechanisms in e-commerce leading to increased perceived economic, relationship-related, and strategic benefits of e-commerce was supported by Siemens. Economic benefits were rated high, because savings in time and costs from ordering online were achieved. A Siemens customer service manager indicated that:

> We experienced economic benefits from reduced telephone calls, as the online extranet application provides a source of information.

Thus, the embedded automated protocols in the extranet applications provided economic benefits. For example, the extranet web site application was only for information access (that is, read-only) and could not be modified or written. Changes and clarifications had to take place via fax or e-mail. Hence, both organizations (Siemens and Telecom NZ) maintained their own private information.

Confidentiality and integrity mechanisms were implemented, thus contributing to relationship-related benefits. Each order contained a Telecom reference number, a Siemens NZ reference number, purchase order number, date received, and date shipped to Telecom, which contributed to a level of transaction integrity that enabled tracking of information. Relationship-related benefits were rated high because of real-time tracking information provided by Mainstream Express. Siemens NZ notified Telecom NZ within 24 hours of the receipt of the order, thus contributing to trading partner satisfaction. A Siemens NZ Key Accounting Manager indicated that:

> We need a couple days to re-order, and inform them of their estimated arrival date. We need to track it, as to when it left the shipping port, from Australia to Munich to Canada where it was manufactured and then shipped back to New Zealand. We undertake regular audits and internal tests and we abide by the British Standards (BS5750) and ISO 9000 for quality.

The findings implied that Siemens enforced best business practices that led to Telecom staff satisfaction. Siemens' sales consultant indicated that:

We exercised best business practices and we received top management commitment. We trained and educated our Telecom staff. Training manuals were made available online.

Siemens NZ and Siemens Australia were jointly awarded the Australian Quality Council Award for progress towards business excellence in November 1999. Both ISO 9002 certification and the progress award provided an indication of Siemens' commitment to continually improve and grow to meet market demands for high-quality and innovative products and services that add value to its customers in NZ. The findings implied that because the Siemens NZ extranet application was hosted on a private server, its security concerns were low. Siemens NZ has put in a lot of effort to maintain its trading partner relationship with Telecom NZ due the competitive environment.

Uni-directional-dyad-8: Telecom NZ R-P: 3
The data suggesting the existence of trust and security-based mechanisms of e-commerce leading to increased perceived economic, relationship-related, and strategic benefits of e-commerce was supported by Telecom. Telecom is a large organization and they have implemented best business practices.

Mainstream express, the Siemens Telecom extranet application that provided real-time tracking information of the orders and product information, contributed to economic benefits from savings in time and costs for telephone calls and e-mails.

Telecom abides by both industry and universal standards and policies. They, too, are ISO 9000 recognized for the Telecom directories. Their technology standard is Telco, which is an industry standard. Other technology trust mechanisms include encryption mechanisms that are carried out via user ID's, log-ons, and passwords. The findings implied that relationship-related and strategic benefits are not supported in this bi-directional dyad.

R-P 4: Technology Trust Mechanisms in E-Commerce are Negatively Associated with Perceived Risks of E-Commerce.
Uni-directional-dyad – 1: NZ Customs R-P: 4
The data suggesting the existence of technology trust mechanisms of e-commerce leading to decreased perceived technology performance-related, relational, and general risks of e-commerce was not supported by NZ

Customs. Most of the risks were rated low to medium. One possible explanation for this is that NZ Customs outsourced part of its customs clearance processes to its ISP, who was responsible for the security of the system. Technology performance-related risks were rated low, as CusMod had embedded mechanisms and protocols that detected all incorrect and incomplete transactions. The findings implied that efficient intelligent testing was implemented to avoid unauthorized log-on procedures or passwords that could interfere with the maintenance and use of technology. Relational risks and general risks did not impact NZ Customs because it received top management support and received directions from the government, thereby enforcing best business practices. The ISP indicated that research proposition four did not apply to them.

Uni-directional-dyad – 3: Customs Broker R-P: 4

The data suggesting that the existence of technology trust mechanisms leading to perceived technology performance-related, relational, and general risks of e-commerce was not supported by the customs broker. The customs broker indicated that:

> General risks were rated low, as we had to abide to the terms and standards of the Customs Act and are involved in a legislative process. We question our importers on their products for correct identity of the goods, and we trust what the importer says as we are making a legal declaration on their behalf. We do not apply segregation of duties, as we are a small company and most of our employees undertake multi-tasks.

The customs broker is aware of the legal implications involved in the customs clearance process and therefore abides by the standards of the Customs Act. The findings implied that employees work as a team and undertake multi-tasks that may contribute to poor business practices because training is only given to staff as and when required.

Uni-directional-dyad – 4: Importer R-P: 4

The data suggesting the existence of technology trust mechanisms in e-commerce leading to perceived technology performance-related, relational, and general risks of e-commerce was not supported by the importer. Most of the risks did not impact the importer and some were rated low because Trade

Manager involves routine, structured business transactions. For example, reference numbers provided unique identification and data integrity, thereby mitigating internal security error. However, the importer was concern about privacy and indicated that:

> Our risks lie in the shipment information being leaked out to other competitors by our customs broker, whom they say sometimes fax documents. The fax revealed the quantity of stock imported for each delivery and can be seen by their employees or any other unauthorized personnel. There are risks in applying poor business practices (lack of audits, back-ups), particularly in a small firm where most of the employees performed multi-tasks.

General risks did not affect the importer because Trade Manager was a separate application used for a specific purpose. The findings implied that the customs' clearance process was separate from other business functions (accounting, human resources, and inventory) in the importer's organization and because the importer enforces best business practices most of the risks were rated low.

Uni-directional-dyad – 5: Cisco NZ R-P: 4
The data suggesting the existence of technology trust mechanisms in e-commerce leading to decreased perceived technology performance-related, relational, and general risks of e-commerce was not supported by Cisco. Cisco NZ found its technology performance-related risks to be low because of its highly sophisticated extranet application and also indicated that most of the risks did not apply to it. Compaq staff only had to log on to Cisco's web site and access product information before placing an order. Hence, compatibility problems with hardware and software were rated low.

Cisco NZ did not emphasize relational or general perceived risks because it exercised good business practices. According to Cisco's Accounting manager:

> One possible explanation for this is our high quality services together with the information we provide (that is timely, accurate) and our IT support group staff are competent, and responsive.

The findings implied that the existence of top management support and commitment at Cisco contributed to low risks.

Uni-directional-dyad – 6: Compaq NZ R-P: 4

The data suggesting the existence of technology trust mechanisms in e-commerce leading to decreased perceived technology performance-related, relational, and general risks of e-commerce was not strongly supported by Compaq NZ. Technology performance-related risks from a lack of compatibility were rated low. Compaq NZ only required an e-mail system and an Internet application to download product information into their systems. However, confidentiality concerns came from an awareness that Cisco staff could send out virus-infected information through their systems. For this reason, Compaq's computer systems had an updated virus scanner. Relational and general risks were rated low, and most of them were not applicable to Compaq NZ because the system was implemented by Cisco.

The findings of this bi-directional dyad implied that although the emphasis was on technology, Compaq staff was aware of the importance of an open and trustworthy trading partner relationship with Cisco NZ.

Uni-directional-dyad – 7: Siemens NZ R-P: 4

The data suggesting the existence of technology trust mechanisms leading to decreased perceived technology performance-related, relational, and general risks of e-commerce was not strongly supported by Siemens NZ. Technology performance-related risks were rated low because the extranet application was hosted on a private server. The speed and provision of on-line tracking information contributed to low relational risks. General risks were rated low because Siemens NZ enforced best business practices.

Uni-directional-dyad – 8: Telecom NZ R-P: 4

The data suggesting the existence of technology trust mechanisms in e-commerce leading to decreased perceived technology performance-related, relational, and general risks of e-commerce was not supported by Telecom. Technology performance-related risks were rated low because the compatibility of e-commerce systems was not a concern, as the extranet application was implemented by one trading partner (the supplier, Siemens). Furthermore, the application was outsourced onto another private server in order to separate public information from private business information. Poor business practices were not an issue for Telecom as it supported a large turnover of staff. Telecom staff indicated that it was a competitive world and a certain amount of turnover or change was good for their organization.

The findings implied that there was a lack of open, trustworthy, and reliable communication between Telecom and Siemens NZ because their business goals were different. For example, Siemens NZ indicated that it was difficult to establish trust because of a high turnover of Telecom staff. On the other hand Telecom staff encouraged the high turnover of staff as they believed that it could bring them quality and skills from new employees.

R-P 5: Perceived Benefits of E-Commerce are Positively Associated with E-Commerce Participation.

Uni-directional-dyad – 1: NZ Customs R-P: 5

The data suggesting the existence of perceived economic, relationship-related, and strategic benefits of e-commerce leading to increased e-commerce participation was strongly supported by NZ Customs. NZ Customs experienced a gradual increase in the volume and dollar value of their business-to-business transactions sent and received using CusMod. NZ Customs relied on e-commerce, as most of their processes involving clearance were automated. 98% of NZ Customs' business was conducted through e-commerce and 92% of it was business-to-business e-commerce. The annual monetary value of e-commerce transactions is NZ $25,574 billion in the year from July 1, 1998 to June 30, 1999. The annual number of e-commerce transactions including both import and export entries was 974,279 transactions for the year 1998-1999, and the operating revenue was NZ $61,254,000. An NZ Customs consultant indicated:

> We represent the nation, and trading partners are definitely our driving forces for adopting e-commerce. NZ Custom's staff conducts regular meetings with industry groups, and conduct business surveys on how CusMod is operating. We have introduced a national call center with a toll-fee number in Auckland where information is made available, free of charge for both importers and exporters. We also have a solid framework (that is a business model) which incorporates government legislative bodies, and builds trust.

> We have moved from a mere gatekeeper for e-commerce transactions to service transactions and business relationships. We try to maintain business continuity and trading partner relationships. Similarly, we perceived an increase in the level of cooperation in our trading partners, as we received support from the government (as in policies to abide). We also perceived an increase in the level of

commitment from our trading partners, as the reputation of our organization increased. Without trust there is no effective communication and without effective communication there is no business-to-business e-commerce.

Hence, NZ Customs experienced an increase in the level of open communication and commitment from its trading partners. The findings also implied that in every aspect, a good level of communication enhances the smooth flow of e-commerce operations, both at a simplistic level and at a complex level. Furthermore, the fact that NZ Customs represented the nation and its mission contributed to its strategic benefits. The ISP indicated that research proposition 5 did not apply to them.

Uni-directional-dyad – 3: Customs Broker R-P: 5

The data suggesting the existence of perceived economic, relationship-related, and strategic benefits of e-commerce leading to increased e-commerce participation was supported by Customs' broker. For example, the customs broker indicated that although only 35% of their business involved the use of Trade Manager, e-commerce was still important. Most of the customs broker's trading partners who were using fax and e-mail to communicate are planning to go on-line. The custom broker's annual monetary value from e-commerce transactions in 1999 was NZ $200,000 (an increase of 10% from 1998). The annual number of e-commerce transactions was 7,200. The use of Trade Manager has increased e-commerce performance for both parties; that in turn helped to build trust and reputation. The customs broker stated that:

> We are now able to compete with the one-stop shop services offered by multi-national freight forwarders and have become a serious competitor for trading partners. Trust is explicit and is built in the trading partner relationship.

The findings implied that trading partner relationships, together with automated e-commerce applications, increased in e-commerce participation.

Uni-directional-dyad – 4: Importer R-P: 5

The data suggesting the existence of perceived economic, relationship-related, and strategic benefits of e-commerce leading to increased e-commerce participation was supported by the importer. E-commerce was important for the importer because it obtained real-time information. There was a definite increase in profitability. Trade Manager facilitated the customs clearance process. Efficiencies from speed, real-time tracking information, electronic clearance, and the reduction in paper work encouraged more orders to be cleared faster and cheaper, thus increasing productivity, profitability, and trading partner satisfaction. According to the importer:

> The annual monetary value of e-commerce transactions in 1999 was NZ$1.5 million (an increase of 15% from 1998). The annual number of e-commerce transactions was 200 input entries that created 600 output entries per year, because each job created between four to five entries.

It can be seen from the findings that risks were more perceived than real. Furthermore, the established long-term relationship between the importer and the customs broker assisted in clarifying uncertainties. The importer defines trust as "being sure that the data input was correct, and not corrupted via viruses or human error".

Uni-directional-dyad – 5: Cisco NZ R-P: 5
The data suggesting the existence of perceived economic, relationship-related, and strategic benefits of e-commerce leading to increased e-commerce participation was strongly supported by Cisco NZ.

Increased e-commerce performance led to economic benefits. After an initial training period, Compaq staff was able to place orders correctly and completely, thereby saving Cisco staff a lot of time clarifying faults. Competence trust along with technology trust mechanisms provided real-time tracking information that led to increased trading partner satisfaction. The Cisco's accounting manager noted that:

> E-commerce is very critical to our organization as it helps reduce the costs and increase customer satisfaction with fewer errors.

Seventy to eighty percent of Cisco's business involved e-commerce, and the annual monetary value of e-commerce transactions is between NZ$17 to 34 billion dollars. The volume of transactions is 2.5 million e-commerce transactions per year. CCO is now selling U.S. $11 million in networking equipment at an annual rate of US $4 billion (Cisco Solutions, 1998). Cisco perceives its organization as engaging in long-term business investments with Compaq NZ. Cisco NZ's sales consultant indicated that:

> Cisco NZ admitted that their number of trading partners has increased. When we first implemented e-commerce on the web we had between 3 to 5 major channel partners, now we have 10 trading partners (channel partners). Our main role is to establish customer preference, and increase the number of channel partners by trading relationship trust, which in turn increases e-commerce participation.

The findings implied that e-commerce success depends on both efficient technologies and well-planned partnerships with mutual goals and trust. Cisco's experience in e-business has set the standard for e-commerce transformation and creating Internet solutions.

Uni-directional-dyad – 6: Compaq NZ R-P: 5

The data suggesting the existence of perceived economic, relationship-related, and strategic benefits of e-commerce leading to increased e-commerce participation was strongly supported by Compaq NZ.

Compaq NZ participants indicated that 80% of their business involved the use of e-commerce and out of that, 20% came from Cisco. The remaining business came from other suppliers. Compaq's annual monetary value of e-commerce transactions in 1999 was NZ$6 million (an increase of 5% since 1998) from 700 annual e-commerce transactions. Compaq NZ's end customers will continue to be a major source of revenue, because Compaq end-consumers demanded Cisco products. There was an increase in the number of trading partners because of the popular demand for Cisco products. Compaq NZ perceives its organization to be engaging in a long-term business relationship with Cisco NZ.

Compaq participants further suggested that Cisco provides high quality services and is committed to be at the top. Cisco claimed that it is number two in the global marketplace. Furthermore, Cisco has been involved in e-commerce for the past twenty years and its standards are universally acceptable. It has a trading partner agreement which outlines procedures, and undertakes regular risk analysis and audit checks. In addition, Cisco provides training and education to Compaq, which it considers very important, thereby contributing to Cisco's high-quality service.

Strategic benefits were implicit because Compaq buys Cisco NZ products, thus helping to build Cisco's image and reputation. Compaq NZ Network specialists indicated that:

> We cannot promise that Cisco was our driving force for adopting e-commerce, as we adopted e-commerce to stay competitive in the business. We have our own web page, products, catalog, and use e-mail with our customers. We, too, have explicit trading agreements with our trading partners' regarding roles and responsibilities and have maintained long-term trading partner relationships with them. We are Cisco's gold trading partner; that is one of Cisco's top ranked trading partners to trade with.

The findings implied that there is an increase in the volume of Compaq's e-commerce performance although trading partner trust relationship development was not obvious. One possible explanation for this is that Compaq NZ was competing with Cisco NZ. Compaq NZ experienced improved organizational image and reputation from better responses, timeliness, and quality of services.

Uni-directional-dyad –7: Siemens NZ R-P: 5
The data suggesting the existence of perceived economic, relationship-related, and strategic benefits of e-commerce leading to increased e-commerce participation was supported by Siemens NZ. The extent of e-commerce performance was rated high, although its extranet application was static (that is, read-only), and served as an information bank to access information.

Siemens NZ's annual monetary value of e-commerce transactions was NZ $15 million in 1999 and its daily number of e-commerce transactions was 400 orders per day. Most orders were worth NZ$1 million and came with smaller parts that had to be re-ordered. A Siemens NZ Marketing manager indicated that:

> Telecom provided Siemens with estimated forecast of supplies required four months ahead.

> We take the risks in relying on the forecast. So far the forecast has been accurate enough but not perfect. Although it is not our preferred way of doing business we have no choice and try to be

flexible. We do hold a buffer stock to meet Telecom NZ urgent orders.

Siemens Marketing manager indicated that:

Our products were complex and we provide a certain amount of selling, in the form of face-to-face meetings with Telecom staff in order to explain the technical components. The widgets need to match the shelf and if Telecom staff ordered the wrong number or size we have to cancel and ask them to re-order by educating them as to what went wrong thus contributing to relationship-related benefits.

Strategic benefits were high because of the uniqueness of the telecommunications products. Siemens participants agreed that e-commerce, in a way, is against relationship building and it is even more difficult for businesses to establish trust due to the lack of human intervention. Reputation, brand name, and image of organization matter a lot, too.

Siemens NZ is working on a relationship charter (Partnering Charter – enclosed in the appendix). The partnering charter is a non-binding contract, which aims to establish positive business relationships, rather than a legal contract. Legal contracts are based on mistrust and suspicion. The relationship charter has three sections: 1) How do trading partners treat vendors? ; 2) How do vendors get served by customers?; and 3) Reciprocal issues such as expecting ethical behaviours from both trading parties. All this is based on initial trust formation. The findings implied that Siemens NZ had put a lot of effort into maintaining its trading partner relationship with Telecom NZ.

Uni-directional-dyad – 8: Telecom NZ R-P: 5
The data suggesting the existence of perceived economic, relationship-related, and strategic benefits of e-commerce leading to increased e-commerce participation was supported by Telecom to a lesser extent. Although 80% of Telecom NZ business involved e-commerce using Siemens NZ's extranet application, Telecom was not impressed. A Telecom NZ participant noted that:

We are interested in solutions not individual items of sale, and encourage our trading partners to think outside the box with sound knowledge. We are in a competitive global environment and have to abide by our trading contract in order to maintain confidential information and intellectual property which allows us to disclose information, and protect our network from being abused and that they can be trusted to solve our problems. Siemens NZ is not totally the driving force for Telecom's e-commerce. Of course we look for speed, simplicity, cost which meets our purpose for undertaking e-commerce. Among other things, that can be on line purchasing and the provision of invoices. Telecom end customers are unaware as to where the technology came from. All they are interested to see is that the phone line works when it needs to.

The findings implied that Siemens NZ wanted the business and an on-going relationship, but Telecom saw it merely as a business transaction.

R-P 6: Perceived Risks of E-Commerce are Negatively Associated with E-Commerce Participation.

Uni-directional-dyad – 1: NZ Customs – R-P: 6

The data suggesting the existence of perceived technology performance-related, relational, and general risks of e-commerce leading to decreased e-commerce participation was not strongly supported by NZ Customs. NZ Customs admitted that it was a big decision for it to outsource part of its e-commerce operations to its ISP. The NZ Customs intranet administrator admitted:

> NZ Customs' concern was about the poor business practices of the ISP that could lead to perceived risks of e-commerce. On the other hand, the time required to train NZ Customs staff to use the new system and manage their 200 trading partners (comprising of exporters, importers, customs brokers, and agents) can create additional administrative time and costs. Although, a cost benefit analysis was seen as critical in e-commerce participation, we realized that establishing a cooperative network of trading partner relationships was even more important for trading partners to communicate, cooperate, and collaborate effectively.

The introduction of the Customs Excise Act in 1996 was vital to NZ Customs' significant modernization. It provided a platform for customs risk management that allowed for greater administrative flexibility and greater transparency in decision-making. NZ Customs' intranet administrator and IT manager indicated:

> All our documents are considered to be legal declarations. NZ Customs' mission is to protect and enhance the interests of the New Zealand community by:
>
> – minimizing the risks that arise from international trade and travel;
>
> – facilitating legitimate movement of people and goods across NZ borders; and
>
> – collecting Customs and excise revenue.

Our services impact the entire nation, passengers traveling out and coming into the country. By and large, businesses aim to make money and provide high quality services that will impact benefits. More importantly, in the customs clearance service, there is a need to collaborate, communicate, and cooperate in order to clear the goods in a timely fashion.

The findings implied that because NZ Customs is an organization that received top management support and strategic directions from the government and is involved in a legislative process, the risks were low. The ISP indicated that research proposition 6 did not apply to it.

Uni-directional-dyad – 3: Customs Broker R-P: 6
The data suggesting the existence of perceived technology performance-related, relational, and general risks of e-commerce leading to decreased e-commerce participation was not strongly supported by the customs broker. The customs broker perceived its risks to be low, as it was not directly competing with its importer. The customs broker was playing the role of a trade facilitator between the importer and NZ Customs.

Uni-directional-dyad – 4: Importer R-P: 6
The data suggesting the existence of perceived technology performance-related, relational, and general risks of e-commerce leading to decreased e-commerce participation was not supported by the importer because Trade Manager was a simple application. Most of the risks were rated low and did

not impact the importer because their business functions were separated from Trade Manager. However, relational risk from a situation of information power leading to functional conflicts was experienced at times, but in most cases these conflicts were solved.

Uni-directional-dyad – 5: Cisco NZ R-P: 6

The data suggesting the existence of perceived technology performance-related, relational, and general risks of e-commerce leading to decreased e-commerce participation was not supported by Cisco. Most of the risks did not impact Cisco because it enforced best business practices and its standards were universally acceptable. Cisco's participants suggested that communicating with e-commerce transactions and paperwork involved in e-commerce adoption was not an issue; however, the business management issues that relied directly on trust behaviours and intentions of trading parties mattered a lot. The findings implied that because Cisco maintained a very good trading partner relationship with Compaq NZ, most of the risks it perceived were low and/or not applicable.

Cisco participants define trust as "information divulged to trading partners that must be kept confidential, and their trading partners must treat them equally, as they treat other business partners and there should be no dirty or under-the-table deals."

Uni-directional-dyad – 6: Compaq NZ R-P: 6

The data suggesting the existence of perceived technology performance-related, relational, and general risks of e-commerce leading to decreased e-commerce participation was not supported by Compaq NZ. Most of the risks did not apply to Compaq NZ and were rated low. There were some relational risks arising from an imbalance of power and most of them related to functional conflicts that did not cause a concern. The findings did not emphasize general risks, as Compaq NZ also implemented best business practices.

Uni-directional-dyad – 7: Siemens NZ R-P: 6

The data suggesting the existence of perceived technology performance-related, relational, and general risks of e-commerce leading to decreased e-commerce participation suggested was difficult for Siemens NZ to establish a stable trading partner trust relationship with Telecom due to a high turnover of staff. Relational risks did exist because Telecom staff felt that they were giving business to Siemens and were misusing their power by demanding a lower price despite the added value in Siemens' products. Most of the general risks were not applicable to Siemens NZ. A Siemens sales consultant indicated that trust is established in a multi-layer relationship in e-commerce. Siemens NZ Sales consultant indicated that:

> We defined trust as being predictable due to consistent behaviors. There should be no surprises to either party, and open dialog. – Siemens NZ Sales Consultant.

The findings implied that Siemens NZ does trust Telecom staff, and the continuation of that trust is based on the continuation of correct behaviour. Technology is only a mechanism for achieving the end goal. E-commerce mechanisms enabled us to meet our end goals. At the end of the day it is the business relationship that counts, not the technology.

Uni-directional dyad-8 – Telecom NZ R-P: 6

The data suggesting the existence of perceived technology performance-related, relational, and general risks of e-commerce leading to reduced e-commerce participation was not supported by Telecom. Telecom participants indicated that sharing of risks was a concern because the extranet application was implemented by Siemens NZ. In fact, technology is counter-productive to relationship building. Organizations should find ways and other means to establish trust in their trading partner relationships (such as face-to-face meetings, telephone, e-mail or fax).

The findings implied that risks did exist, although it was implicit. General risks did not impact Telecom's participation in e-commerce as they exercised best business practices in the form of high quality standards and services.

DISCUSSION: CROSS-CASE ANALYSIS OF THE BI-DIRECTIONAL DYADS

Miles and Huberman (1994) suggest that cross-case analysis enhances generalization and deepens understanding. This section discusses the findings from a cross-case analysis of eight uni-directional dyads (organizations) that formed four bi-directional dyads.

R-P 1: Trading Partner Trust is Positively Associated with Perceived Benefits of E-Commerce.

The impact of competence, predictability, and goodwill trading partner trust on perceived economic, relationship-related, and strategic benefits was strongly supported by most of the bi-directional dyads. Table 19 provides a summary of the impact of trading partner trust on perceived benefits of e-commerce. Competence trust was rated high by most of the bi-directional dyads except for bi-directional dyad D (Siemens-Telecom NZ). One possible explanation for this could be that in Siemens-Telecom NZ dyad, the impact on economic benefits was rated low to medium. Siemens NZ outsourced a private server for its extranet application. The increased turnover of Telecom staff created difficulties for Siemens staff as they had to re-train the new staff. In addition, the complexity of the parts and the lack of knowledge and expertise about the products led to uncertainties when placing an order. On the other hand, Telecom's end customers were unaware or were not concerned as to where the parts for their mobile phones or telecommunication equipment came from as long as the equipment worked.

In the case of NZ Customs and its ISP (bi-directional dyad A) the ability of its trading partners to use e-commerce applications correctly after an initial period of making mistakes made it realize economic benefits (i.e., savings from time and costs in re-sending the same transaction twice). The findings show that although NZ Customs did provide initial support to its importers and exporters, it can be a complex area for new trading partners. Furthermore, NZ Customs received support from the government, and had the financial resources and top management commitment to outsource part of its business-to-business e-commerce processes to its Internet Service Provider. In bi-directional dyad B, both the customs broker and the importer were two small organizations that applied a user-friendly Microsoft application, Trade Manager. The automated clearance process led to fewer errors, and transactions were cleared more quickly, thus contributing to economic benefits from savings in time and cost for the importer. In addition, the customs broker provided free software installation and training for the importer, who experienced relationship-related benefits from the past experiences it had with the customs broker. With Cisco-Compaq NZ (bi-directional dyad C), competence trust was rated medium to high because although Cisco NZ, being the world's leader of e-commerce, had powerful and sophisticated tools with embedded checking mechanisms that detected errors made by Compaq, initial mistakes and training was observed. The process involved in creating an order for the products and components was a complex one. Furthermore, Cisco NZ's Internet Business Solutions group managed all queries about technical difficulties and clarifications through its extranet application (Cisco Connection Online). Although Compaq has been using CCO for the past eighteen months, Compaq had a trading partner relationship with Cisco for the past ten years. It can be seen that the focus may point towards the fact that a high level of competence trust, technology and financial resources, and relationships (such as honesty in providing reliable information) were found to be important. They were able to accomplish on-line what used to be done over the telephone and e-mail. The time saving allowed them to concentrate on strategic planning (goodwill trust), which contributed to economic, relationship-related, and strategic benefits.

Although the technology initially contributed to economic benefits, one can argue that trading partners continued to trade for long periods of time (ten to fifteen years) even before the e-commerce technologies were implemented that contributed to trading partner satisfaction.

The findings implied that trading partner trust was found to be important by most of the bi-directional dyads because the ability, skills, and competence of trading partners were essential for successful e-commerce participation. Even though trading partners were trading with each other prior to adopting e-commerce applications, they agreed that although the automation of e-commerce technologies provided the speed, quality, and timely information, training trading partners was found to be even more important. Consistent, positive

Table 19: Research Proposition 1 – Trading partner trust and perceived benefits of e-commerce

Three Types of Trading Partner Trust	Bi-directional Dyad A NZ Customs and their ISP Directional Dyads 1-2	Bi-directional Dyad B Customs Broker And Importer Directional Dyads 3-4	Bi-directional Dyad C Cisco NZ and Compaq NZ Directional Dyads 5-6	Bi-directional Dyad D Siemens NZ and Telecom NZ Directional Dyads 7-8
Competence Trust Economic benefits	H	H	M-H	L-M
Predictability Trust Relationship-related benefits	H	H	H	H
Goodwill Trust Relationship-related and strategic benefits	M	H	M	M-H

Legend: L = Low (0-3); M = Medium (4-6); H - High (7-10).

competence trust demonstrated by trading partners' ability to transact correctly contributed to predictability trust and trading partner satisfaction, which in turn led to goodwill trust in the form of increased honesty, open communications, cooperation, commitment to long-term trading partner relationships, and reputation. Thus, it can be concluded from the findings that trading partner trust was important as it contributed to economic benefits of e-commerce. Then perceived relationship-related benefits were derived from consistent positive competence trust that led to predictability trust. In the long run this led to strategic benefits from closer ties and commitment to long-term investments. Table 19 below presents the impact of trading partner trust on perceived benefits of e-commerce.

R-P 2: Trading Partner Trust is Negatively Associated with Perceived Risks of E-Commerce.

The impact of competence, predictability, and goodwill trading partner trust on perceived technology performance-related, relational, and general risks was not strongly supported by most of the bi-directional dyads. Table 20 presents the impact of trading partner trust on perceived risks of e-commerce. Most e-commerce systems and applications were user-friendly and came with standardized routines using a set of menu options that contributed to low technology-performance related risks. The risks derived from a lack of competence were rated low by most of the bi-directional dyads. Bi-directional dyad A (NZ Customs) rated technology performance-related risks to be low because it had outsourced part of its business-to-business e-commerce process to its Internet Service Provider, who could exhibit opportunistic behaviours derived from expert knowledge that contributed to relational risks. Bi-directional dyad C (Cisco-Compaq) rated technology performance-related risks to be low because CCO was only implemented by Cisco, and Compaq staff only had to log on to the web site using authorization mechanisms. Similarly, Siemens-Telecom NZ (bi-directional dyad D) rated technology performance-related risks to be low because they, too, had outsourced their extranet application to a private server. However, they rated relational risks to be medium due to a lack of predictability trust arising from a high turnover of staff. Telecom staff, on the other hand, also rated technology performance-related risks to be low because they had to log on to a private server.

The findings implied that relational risks were rated low to medium by the importer (bi-directional dyad B) because it was suspicious that its customs broker exercised poor business practices. The importer faxed invoices that revealed its details, prices of goods, and types and quantity of the goods ordered to the customs broker.

General risks were rated low and were not applicable by most of the bi-directional dyads because of the implementation of best business practices (including audits, backups, high quality, standards, and training). The findings provided evidence that trading partner trust does impact risk. Trading partner relationship trust contributed to low risks in most of the directional dyads. Most of the bi-directional dyads rated the impact of technology performance-related risks to be very important.

Relational risks and general risks arising from poor business practices were considered very important by all the bi-directional dyads. Abiding to high quality standards and procedures was expected from the organizations. Trading partners had to impress each other in order to build their reputation and image, thereby building goodwill trust. The findings concluded that the bi-directional dyads recognized the importance and impact of risks of e-commerce, and that every possible action was taken to enforce best business practices (e.g., implementing regular training programs) that help build competence trust. Table 20 presents the impact of trading partner trust on perceived risks of e-commerce.

Table 20: Research Proposition 2 – Trading partner trust and perceived risks of e-commerce

Three Types of Trading Partner Trust	Bi-directional Dyad A NZ Customs and their ISP Directional dyads 1-2	Bi-directional Dyad B Customs Broker and Importer Directional dyads 3-4	Bi-directional Dyad C Cisco NZ and Compaq NZ Directional Dyads 5-6	Bi-directional Dyad D Siemens NZ and Telecom NZ Directional dyads 7-8
Competence Trust Technology performance-related risks	L-M	L-M	L	L
Predictability Trust Relational risks	M-H	L-M	L	M
Goodwill Trust General risks	N/A	N/A	L-N/A	L-N/A

Legend: L = Low (0-3); M = Medium (4-6); H – High (7-10).

R-P 3: Technology Trust Mechanisms in E-Commerce are Positively Associated with Perceived Benefits of E-Commerce.

The impact of technology trust mechanisms on perceived economic, relationship-related, and strategic benefits of e-commerce was strongly supported by most of the bi-directional dyads. Table 21 presents the impact of technology trust mechanisms on perceived benefits. Most of the bi-directional dyads rated perceived benefits to be high because the main goal of e-commerce systems and applications was to provide efficiency, thus contributing to economic benefits. Bi-directional dyad A (NZ Customs) rated perceived economic benefits to be high because the CusMod system had embedded automated checking mechanisms and protocols that enabled detection of errors. Furthermore, its ISP provided the technical expertise, compatible systems, training, and support that help build relational benefits. On the other hand, the customs broker and importer rated perceived benefits to be medium to high for reasons of confidentiality, access controls, and best business practices. One possible explanation for this is that their e-commerce application Trade Manager was not attached to their network. Most of the bi-directional dyads experienced benefits from technology trust mechanisms because of their initial investments in implementing e-commerce, as they were able to provide adequate training and ensure that their systems were secure and met their business requirements and high quality standards. In the case of bi-directional dyad C, Cisco NZ's extranet application was a powerful tool with embedded checking mechanisms that detected and corrected errors, contributing to economic benefits from savings in time and cost. Similarly, Compaq too gained from the on-line tracking of information that was made available from the time an order was placed until the goods were delivered. Consistent achievement of economic benefits led to relationship-related benefits from trading partner satisfaction. In the case of bi-directional dyad D (Siemens-Telecom NZ), they, too, experienced economic benefits from savings in time and cost as product information was made available on their extranet application. Siemens extranet web site application was only for information access (i.e., read only) and could not be modified or written.

The findings provided evidence that technology trust mechanisms enabled trading partner trust to be developed and implied that its impact on perceived benefits were rated very important by most of the bi-directional dyads. Most of the technology trust mechanisms were related to security principles (such as confidentiality, integrity, authenticity, non-repudiation, availability, and access

Table 21: Research Proposition 3 – Technology trust mechanisms and perceived benefits of e-commerce

Technology trust mechanisms in E-commerce	Bi-directional Dyad A NZ Customs and their ISP Directional dyads 1-2	Bi-Directional Dyad B Customs Broker And Importer Directional dyads 3-4	Bi-directional Dyad C Cisco NZ and Compaq NZ Directional dyads 5-6	Bi-directional Dyad D Siemens NZ and Telecom NZ Directional dyads 7-8
Confidentiality Economic benefits	H	M	H	H
Integrity Economic benefits	H	H	H	H
Authentication Relationship-related benefits	H	H	H	H
Non-repudiation Relationship-related benefits	H	H	H	H
Availability Economic benefits	H	M	H	H
Access Controls Economic benefits	H	M	H	H
Best Business Practices Relationship-related and strategic benefits	H	M	H	H

Legend: L = Low (0-3); M = Medium (4-6); H - High (7-10).

controls), so measures were taken to include these mechanisms into their e-commerce systems and applications (as protocols). For example, a simple e-mail acknowledgment followed by a telephone call confirmed that trading partners were communicating to the right trading party. Top management commitment (as in adequate and regular audits, a formal development methodology, risk management, and contingency procedures) ensured high-quality services and contributed to economic and relationship-related benefits. The findings concluded that e-commerce technologies had embedded protocols that contributed to economic benefits of e-commerce (i.e., the findings recognized the importance of technology trust). In addition, consistent enforcement of best business practices led to relationship-related and strategic benefits as high quality standards and written policies were implemented. Table 21 presents the impact of technology trust mechanisms on perceived benefits of e-commerce.

R-P 4: Technology Trust Mechanisms in E-Commerce are Negatively Associated with Perceived Risks of E-Commerce.

The impact of technology trust mechanisms on perceived technology performance-related, relational, and general risks of e-commerce was not strongly supported by most of the bi-directional dyads. Table 22 presents the impact of technology trust mechanisms on perceived risks of e-commerce. Technology trust mechanisms in e-commerce and their impact on perceived risks were rated low by all the organizations because the compatibility of the systems was not an issue between trading partners in a dyad. Furthermore, there were efficiencies from e-commerce applications that came with embedded security mechanisms. These mechanisms enabled errors to be quickly detected and corrected, saving a lot of time transmitting e-commerce transactions. For example, in bi-directional A (NZ Customs-ISP) intelligent testing was implemented to eliminate unauthorized log-on procedures or passwords that could interfere with the maintenance and use of technology.

Most of the technology trust mechanisms were not applicable for bi-directional dyad B (Customs Broker-Importer), because the Customs broker is aware of the legal implications involved in the customs clearance process and therefore abides by the standards of the Customs Act. However, the importer was concerned about confidentiality of its shipment information being leaked out to other competitors by the customs broker because of poor business practices. Cisco NZ found its technology performance-related risks to be low because of its highly sophisticated extranet application and also indicated that most of the risks did not apply to it. Avery Ford NZ and Toyota NZ, because their e-commerce applications were simple, user-friendly systems and information was internally distributed. Cisco NZ found its technology performance-related risks to be low because of its highly sophisticated extranet application, and both Cisco NZ and Compaq NZ indicated that most of the risks did not apply to them. Furthermore, high quality standards were practiced. In bi-directional dyad D, Telecom NZ rated technology performance-related risks to be low because the compatibility of e-commerce systems was not a concern, as the extranet application was implemented by the trading partner (Siemens NZ). The findings provided evidence of three factors. First, efficiencies of e-commerce technologies and applications reduced compatibility problems and technology performance-related risks. Second, due to past experience, relational risks were rated low as the organizations knew who they were dealing with. Most of the bi-directional dyads enforced best business practices and had to abide by industry standards that provided high quality services that contributed to low general risks.

The findings implied that technology trust mechanisms and its impact on perceived risks of e-commerce were rated very important by all the bi-directional dyads. Although a lack of these mechanisms may contribute to technology performance-related risks from incompatibility of e-commerce

Table 22: Research Proposition 4 – Technology trust mechanisms and perceived risks of e-commerce

Technology trust mechanisms in E-commerce	Bi-directional Dyad A NZ Customs and their ISP Directional dyads 1-2	Bi-Directional Dyad B Customs Broker And Importer Directional dyads 3-4	Bi-directional Dyad C Cisco NZ and Compaq NZ Directional dyads 5-6	Bi-directional Dyad D Siemens NZ and Telecom NZ Directional dyads 7-8
Confidentiality Technology performance-related risks	L	M	L	L
Integrity Technology performance-related risks	L-M	L	L	L
Authentication Relational risks	N/A	L	L	L
Non-repudiation Relational risks	N/A	L	L	L
Availability Technology performance and Relational risks	N/A	L	L	L
Access Controls Technology performance-related risks	L	N/A	L	L
Best Business Practices General risks	N/A	L	N/A	L

Legend: L = Low (0-3); M = Medium (4-6); H - High (7-10). Not Applicable

applications in the short-run, they may also contribute to relational and general risks in the long run. Furthermore, a lack of top management commitment could lead to poor business practices that inhibit trading partners from being fully trained to undertake e-commerce operations correctly. This in turn could lead to integrity risks as e-commerce transactions sent by trading partners may be incomplete and inaccurate. Trading partner dissatisfaction derived from a lack of competence could lead to opportunistic behaviours, conflicts, and discontinuity of trading partner relationships. The findings concluded that the more time spent on planning and enforcing technology trust mechanisms may lead to decreased risks of e-commerce, as trading partners were trained to use e-commerce systems properly, thereby making less errors and providing fewer opportunities for hackers. Table 22 presents the impact of technology trust mechanisms on perceived risks of e-commerce.

R-P 5: Perceived Benefits of E-Commerce are Positively Associated with E-Commerce Participation.

The impact of perceived economic, relationship-related, and strategic benefits on the outcomes of e-commerce participation was strongly supported by most of the bi-directional dyads. Table 23 presents the impact of perceived benefits of e-commerce on the extent of e-commerce participation. One possible explanation for this is the automation and speed that e-commerce applications provided increased e-commerce performance, thus contributing to economic benefits. Most of the e-commerce operations involved standardized routine processes. Most of the trading partners were trading manually or used other means of communicating before trading with e-commerce applications. Furthermore, trading partners have met each other before. Bi-directional dyad A (NZ Customs-ISP) represents the nation, and 98% of their business was conducted electronically. Economic benefits in bi-directional dyad B were rated medium because the customs broker only acted as a trade facilitator and was not directly involved in the importing and distribution of the products or goods. The importer found e-commerce important for it because it received real-time information. Similarly, strategic benefits and their impact on e-commerce participation were rated medium by the importer. In bi-directional dyad C, seventy to eighty percent of Cisco's business involved e-commerce. Compaq NZ indicated that twenty percent of its e-commerce comes from Cisco. Compaq's findings indicated an increase in e-commerce performance, although trading partner trust relationship development was not obvious because Compaq was competing with Cisco NZ. Siemens rated strategic benefits to be high because of the uniqueness of the telecommunication products. Telecom NZ bi-directional dyad D rated relationship-related and strategic benefits to be medium because their end-customers were unaware as to who actually manufactured the parts of their product.

The findings implied that perceived economic benefits and their impact on the extent of e-commerce participation was rated very important by all the bi-directional dyads except NZ Customs. One possible explanation for this is that NZ Customs is a public sector service organization supported by the government. Its main goal was to provide customs clearance services for the country, and not to engage in fierce competition to make high profits. The other bi-directional dyads experienced economic benefits from savings in costs and time derived from the automated e-commerce processes. Economic benefits led to perceived indirect benefits that paved the way for trading partner trust relationship development, which was very important for e-commerce applications to operate on a real-time round the clock basis, thus making information readily available and accessible. Consistent competence trading partner trust behaviours were important for organizations to manage their supply chain activities, thus leading to predictability trust. Increased satisfaction among trading partners led to relationship-related benefits that permitted trading

Table 23: Research Proposition 5 – Perceived benefits of e-commerce and the outcomes of e-commerce participation

Perceived Benefits of E-commerce	Bi-directional Dyad A NZ Customs and their ISP Directional dyads 1-2	Bi-directional Dyad B Customs Broker and Importer Directional dyads 3-4	Bi-directional Dyad C Cisco NZ and Compaq NZ Directional Dyads 5-6	Bi-directional Dyad D Siemens NZ and Telecom NZ Directional dyads 7-8
Perceived economic benefits Extent of E-commerce Performance	H	M-H	H	H
Perceived relationship-related benefits of E-commerce Extent of trading partner trust relationship development	H	H	H	M
Perceived strategic benefits Extent of trading partner trust relationship development	H	M	H	M-H

Legend: L = Low (0-3); M = Medium (4-6); H - High (7-10). Not Applicable

partners to share information, and have open communications and increased commitment. This in turn gradually led to strategic benefits that contributed to increased e-commerce performance, long-term trading relationships, increased reputation of trading partners, and trading partner trust relationship development. The findings concluded that the importance of trading partner trust encouraged consistent open communications among trading partners, and a willingness to share information which led to positive feelings. Table 23 presents the impact of perceived benefits of e-commerce and the extent of e-commerce participation.

R-P 6: Perceived Risks of E-Commerce are Negatively Associated with E-Commerce Participation.

The impact of perceived technology performance-related, relational, and general risks of e-commerce and their impact on the extent of e-commerce participation were not strongly supported by most of the directional-dyads. Table 24 presents the impact of perceived risks on e-commerce participation. The impact of perceived risks on the extent of e-commerce participation was rated low by most of the bi-directional dyads, except for the Siemens-Telecom NZ, which rated the impact of perceived risks on e-commerce participation to be medium. One possible explanation for this is that the ordering process was a complex one. Furthermore, the high turnover of staff by Telecom created added difficulties for Siemens NZ, as it had to re-train its new staff all over again. Thus a lack of consistent competence trust demonstrated from Telecom staff created a situation of dissatisfaction and contributed to relational and general risks. Most of the risks did not impact bi-directional dyad C (Cisco-Compaq NZ), because they enforced best business practices and their standards were universally acceptable. In the case of NZ Customs, the Customs Excise Act was vital to its significant modernization and customs risk management. Most of the risks did not impact bi-directional dyad C (Cisco-Compaq) because they enforced best business practices and their standards were universally acceptable. On the whole the findings provided evidence that perceived risks to e-commerce were not strongly supported by other bi-directional dyads.

The findings implied that perceived risks of e-commerce and their impact on the outcomes of e-commerce participation was rated very important by all bi-directional dyads except for uni-directional dyads. Trading partners who constantly exhibit mistakes can cause delays in the supply chain management. This in turn could affect trading partner satisfaction and trading partner trust relationship development, thus contributing to relational risks. Opportunistic behaviours from an imbalance of power can inhibit open communications and information sharing that could affect trading partner trust relationship develop-

Table 24: Research Proposition 6 – Perceived risks of e-commerce and outcomes of e-commerce participation

Perceived Risks of E-commerce	Bi-directional Dyad A NZ Customs and their ISP Directional dyads 1-2	Bi-directional Dyad B Customs Broker and Importer Directional dyads 3-4	Bi-directional Dyad C Cisco NZ and Compaq NZ Directional Dyads 5-6	Bi-directional Dyad D Siemens NZ and Telecom NZ Directional dyads 7-8
Perceived technology performance related risks Extent of E-commerce Performance	L	L	L-N/A	M
Perceived relational risks Extent of trading partner trust relationship development	L	L	L	M
Perceived general risks Extent of E-commerce participation and trading partner trust relationship development	L	M	L-N/A	M

Legend: L = Low (0-3); M = Medium (4-6); H - High (7-10). Not Applicable

ment and ultimately their business continuity. The findings concluded that all bi-directional dyads recognized the importance of perceived risks of e-commerce as they can directly affect participation in e-commerce. Table 24 presents the impact of perceived risks on e-commerce participation.

The next section discusses the similarities and differences in the bi-directional dyads.

SIMILARITIES AND DIFFERENCES OF THE BI-DIRECTIONAL DYADS

The similarities and differences in the findings came from the type of industry and e-commerce applications used. Organizations that implemented extranet applications (Cisco-Compaq NZ and Siemens-Telecom NZ) had to deal with complex parts and a difficult ordering process. Furthermore, the implementation of the e-commerce extranet application was carried out by only one trading party (i.e., the supplier – Cisco NZ and Siemens NZ), who is responsible for updating it with real-time tracking information of the products and orders placed by its buyers. These initial one-sided implementation costs motivated suppliers at times to apply coercive power and exhibit opportunistic behaviours (in the form of high prices) to their buyers, thus contributing to relational risks of e-commerce.

The similarities between NZ Customs and the customs broker and importer were long-term trading partner relationships. The impact of e-commerce participation by smaller organizations such as the customs broker and importer was successful. One possible explanation for this was the simplicity of their e-commerce application, and because for security reasons their e-commerce application was not connected to the networks. The differences between NZ Customs and its Internet Service Provider include outsourcing part of its e-commerce processes to its Internet Service Provider.

In this chapter, we discussed the findings of the eight uni-directional dyads that formed four bi-directional dyads. We presented the background for each company and then discussed the findings based on each research proposition, followed by a cross-case analysis of the findings that presented the importance, similarities, and differences of the findings. In the next chapter, we conclude the study by contributing to a model of inter-organizational trust within bi-directional dyads and discuss the implications of the study to theory and practice.

Chapter VI

Conclusions

In this chapter we conclude our study by contributing to a model of inter-organizational trust within bi-directional dyads based on the findings of this study. The participants agreed that technology trust mechanisms (also known as technology trust) by and large exist in e-commerce technologies and applications. Technology trust is defined as *"the subjective probability by which an organization believes that the underlying technology infrastructure and control mechanisms are capable of facilitating inter-organizational transactions according to its confident expectations"* (Ratnasingam and Pavlou, 2002, 2003). However, what is more important is the need to develop trading partner relationships that will form cohesive (win-win) trading partner relationships. Most of the participants agreed that developing trust is a gradual process and can be challenging because of differing personalities and expectations, the lack of a physical presence, varied standards used within each organization, and the changing external e-commerce environment. The rest of the chapter is organized as follows. The next section presents and discusses the model of inter-organizational trust within bi-directional dyads. Then we discuss the contributions to theory and practice, leading to the limitations of the study and recommendations for future research.

MODEL OF INTER-ORGANIZATIONAL TRUST WITHIN BI-DIRECTIONAL DYADS IN E-COMMERCE PARTICIPATION

The model of inter-organizational trust within bi-directional dyads in e-commerce participation was developed from the findings. The model identifies the gradual development of inter-organizational trust in three stages. Table 26 outlines the characteristics of the three stages of inter-organizational trust. Figure 8 depicts the model of inter-organizational trust within bi-directional dyads in e-commerce participation.

Although business-to-business e-commerce systems and applications facilitate the development of initial competence trust, trust needs time to develop, as it evolves gradually from one stage to the next stage. The model enables trading partners to identify which stage of trust they and their trading partners belong to. In the first stage, new e-commerce adopters typically concentrate on training their trading partners to use e-commerce applications correctly, thus taking a bottom up approach in analyzing trust behaviours (such

Figure 8: Model of inter-organizational trust within bi-directional dyads in e-commerce participation

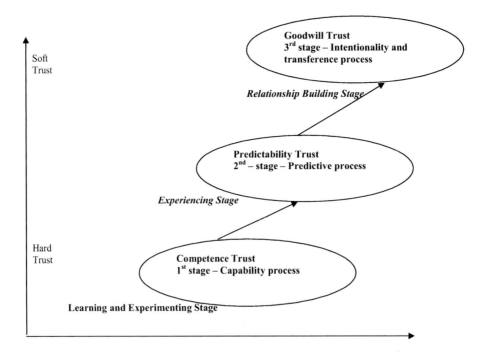

as trading partner skills, knowledge, ability, and product expertise). The emphasis is on the trading partners' competence, skills, and ability to operate business-to-business e-commerce applications. The first stage of inter-organizational trust development contributes to transactional (objective) trust, and focuses on a capability process which examines how trading partners send and receive business-to-business e-commerce transactions (i.e., trading partners' competence). This contributes to economic benefits from high competence trust, and also from trust and security-based mechanisms (as automated protocols) embedded in e-commerce technologies that provide speed and real-time accurate information. Economic benefits are derived from savings in time and costs as trading partners are able to send and receive transactions correctly. Alternatively, trading partners who operate using incompatible e-commerce applications or apply poor business practices (as in inadequate audit, lack of training) and constantly make errors during transacting contribute to technology performance-related risks.

During the second stage, consistent positive behaviours from trading partners lead to credibility and reliability. Positive behaviours from reliable trading partners contribute to trustworthy behaviours and predictability trust. This, in turn, increases trading partner satisfaction and contributes to relationship-related benefits such as open communication and a willingness to cooperate, commit, and share information. The predictive process applies a middle-out approach for analyzing trust behaviours of trading partners because it is based on knowledge of past experiences. The focus gradually evolves from transactional (objective) trust to relational (subjective) trust that emphasizes trading partners' behaviours (such as reliability, honesty, and predictability). Alternatively, trading partners who do not exhibit consistent, reliable, positive trust contribute to relational risks derived from uncertainties, lack of knowledge, dependencies, situations of imbalance of power, and conflicts.

Finally, in the third stage, goodwill trust focuses on institutional (organizational) reputation and brand names, accomplished by enforcing best business practices. Positive consistent behaviours encourage trading partners to invest in their trading partner relationships (i.e., renew the trading partners' contract), increase e-commerce performance (as in volume, dollar value of goods), and reduce opportunistic behaviours (such as power, control, and the imposition of strict deadlines). Thus, positive repeated behaviours from trading partners enable goodwill trust to develop, which is an accumulation of both competence and predictability trust. The focus is on the organization and it takes a top-down approach in analyzing trading partner trust behaviours. This approach includes top management commitment, high-quality standards, open communication, information sharing, and long-term trading partner relationships, thus contributing to strategic benefits. Alternatively, poor business practices (such as a lack of audit reviews or top management commitment) may lead to general risks. Research on trust has shown that trust is transferable, thus trust in this stage is based on a transference process (see Doney and Cannon, 1997; Lewicki and Bunker, 1995). Table 25 presents trust behaviours and characteristics of bi-directional dyads in e-commerce participation.

It can be concluded that inter-organizational trust is important for e-commerce participation. The model of inter-organizational trust within bi-directional dyads in e-commerce participation identified characteristics that determined positive and negative consequences of inter-organizational trust. E-commerce practitioners will benefit from this information, as they will be able to assess the likely effects and effectiveness of trust if applied correctly in their organization. This study contributed to the determinants of successful e-commerce participation.

Table 25: Model of inter-organizational trust within bi-directional dyads in e-commerce participation

Three Stages of Inter-Organizational Trust	Bi-directional Dyads A-D (Supplier)	Bi-directional dyads A-D (Buyer)
Competence based Trust (Economic Foundation) (win-lose situation)	- Enforces trading partner agreement - Provides initial training - Exhibits tolerance for mistakes. Applies persuasive power - Focuses on operational goals - Emphasizes trust and security-based mechanisms from e-commerce applications	- Experiments with new e-commerce applications - Makes costly mistakes - Experiences an increase in communication and trading partner interactions (via telephone calls, email, and fax) - Relies on IT technical support - Experiences economic benefits -Experiences technology performance related risks
Predictability based Trust (Familiarity Foundation) (could be win-lose, lose-win, win-win, or lose-lose situation)	- Consistent behaviours in providing high quality service - Focuses on mid-range tactical goals - Experiences relationship-related benefits from trading partner satisfaction - Experiences relational risks	- Experiences the ability to operate correctly from previous mistakes - Exhibits consistent behaviour - Experiences both economic and relationship-related benefits - Experiences relational risks - End consumers exhibit satisfaction
Goodwill based Trust (Empathy Foundation) (win-win situation)	- Increases reputation of their organization - Brand names - Aims to sign long-term contracts - Plans strategic long-term goals - Experiences increase in e-commerce performance (that is, increased volume, dollar value of goods) - Exhibits less opportunistic behaviour - Experiences increase in trading partner trust - Exhibits willingness to share information, open communication	- Exhibits cooperation - Exhibits commitment - Experiences an increase in trading partner satisfaction - Exhibits willingness to put every effort to invest in the relationship - Experiences strategic benefits and increased reputation - Engages in long-term investments

RESEARCH CONTRIBUTIONS AND IMPLICATIONS

This section discusses the contributions (to theory and business practices) and implications of this study.

Contributions to Theory

The first contribution came from an insight to successfully bridge the ideas about trust from multiple disciplines. The integrated conceptual model tested in this study was developed from the findings of the exploratory study and the basis of several well-established theories from many fields discussed. They include marketing, management, sociology, information systems, and e-commerce literature. The model was complete, as it included both the strengths and weaknesses of both trading partner trust and trust and security-based mechanisms (technology trust). The five theoretical perspectives include:

- inter-organizational relationship theory;

- transaction-cost-economics theory;

- resource dependency theory;

- theories of trust in business relationships; and

- theories from computer science and information systems literature relating to trust and security-based mechanisms in e-commerce.

Although information systems research relating to trading partner trust in e-commerce participation was limited, past research on trust in business relationships from other disciplines pointed towards the importance of trust in business relationships. A synthesis of the above theories provided a new approach for exploring, studying, and describing inter-organizational trust relationships in e-commerce participation. Previous research on e-commerce mostly focused on technological benefits and its competitive advantages. This study not only examined the technological perspective, but also behavioural, economical, organizational, and socio-political perspectives of trading partners. The constructs in the conceptual model were adequate to conceptualize, describe, and empirically examine inter-organizational trust in e-commerce participation.

The second contribution to theory is the importance of the actual topic. Trust in e-commerce participation has received a lot of attention, especially in the recent years. The findings of this research provide evidence that technology alone is insufficient for successful e-commerce participation. Trading partner trust provides an avenue for increasing the understanding of bi-directional dyads in e-commerce participation.

The third contribution came from a cross-industry selection of organizations and the perspectives of both the trustor and trustee that participated in this study. Most previous research only examined trading partner trust from either a supplier's or buyer's perspective, or from one type of industry. This study examined trading partner trust from both trading partners' perspectives (i.e., buyer-supplier; trustor-trustee) within a bi-directional dyad. This study is unique, as inter-organizational trust was examined in ten uni-directional dyads (organizations) from a cross-section of industries, namely, telecommunications, computer and data communication supply, customs clearance (including an Internet service provider, importer, and customs broker), automotive dealers, and distributors that formed four bi-directional dyads (bi-directional dyads A-D).

The fourth contribution is the model of inter-organizational trust within bi-directional dyads in e-commerce participation (see Figure 8). The model identifies the development of inter-organizational trust in three stages, and it allows trading partners to identify which stage of trust they and their trading partners belong to. The model shows a gradual development of trust from one stage to the next stage, thus providing an awareness of the trust behaviours that trading partners need to develop. For example, competence trust emphasizes an individual or team's ability and skills to operate e-commerce systems and applications. Predictability trust examined the reflections and interpersonal experiences of the trading partners based on past experiences, and goodwill trust examined the institutional (i.e., the organization's image and reputation) that determined the strategic benefits.

Contributions to Practice

This study has the potential to provide practitioners with insights to acknowledge the importance of different trust behaviours in their business relationships in the following ways.

First, a key strength of the research is that the respondents were practitioners from a wide range of organizations and occupations. Therefore, while the participating organizations and their people were not selected randomly, quite a diverse group did participate.

Second, the participants of this study agreed that this study increased their awareness that inter-organizational trust relationships are worthy of inclusion in the production of their future audit reports, guidelines, and security policies. Organizations should participate in industry working groups, thus increasing their awareness of security requirements, e-commerce methods of operations, and interchange standards. Participation in industry groups provides an indication of the organization's commitment and plan towards e-commerce participation. For example, automotive manufacturers conduct regular discussions with key management personnel, thus allowing formal approvals and links in a realistic setting that encourages e-commerce participation. By doing so, their awareness of trading partner trust will increase, thereby enabling trading partners to sustain and commit to long-term trading partner relationships. E-commerce organizations will be able to practice business-to-business e-commerce more confidently, as they will be made aware of the trust behaviours.

Third, this study provides a guide for early developers and implementers of business-to-business e-commerce by improving and increasing their levels of awareness of the potential use of e-commerce technology. Trading partners will be made aware of the importance of inter-organizational trust in their trading partner relationships, thereby helping e-commerce organizations to improve their chances of surviving in a competitive global market environment.

Fourth, experienced e-commerce practitioners (trading partners) will be able to observe the behaviours of their trading partners and will be able to monitor, assess, and evaluate antecedent trust behaviours of themselves and their trading partners. By doing so, they can determine the extent of their trading partners' trustworthiness and will be able to protect themselves against fraud on the opportunistic, suspicious behaviours of their trading partners. Although governance mechanisms (including legal contracts, trust and security-based mechanisms in e-commerce) provide technological assurances (using digital signatures, encryption mechanisms, functional acknowledgment procedures, and trading partner agreements) that help mitigate perceived risks of e-commerce, the findings provided evidence that inter-organizational trust is still the key to sustained long-term relationships.

Finally, this study contributes to the importance of inter-organizational trust in e-commerce participation by developing an integrated framework describing the role of trust and technology (security mechanisms) in participation in e-commerce. The framework was tested through multiple case studies. The findings contributed to a model of inter-organizational trust within bi-directional dyads in e-commerce participation. The model of inter-organizational trust within bi-directional dyads in e-commerce participation thus acts as a checking mechanism for both growth and development of inter-organizational trust in business-to-business e-commerce participation. Therefore, the contributions to practice focused on:

*   designing and implementing an effective trading contract (that emphasizes a partnering contract) rather than a trading contract;

*   designing a pre-adoption education and training program in order to develop competence trust of trading partners. For example, Stewart (1998) suggests building trust in e-commerce by educating trading partners and ensuring security, privacy of transactions, and protection of trading partners. Trading partners should establish ground rules so that commercial laws, tax and customs tariffs, trade policies, market access, and intellectual property measures create a universal standard for electronic transactions. This enhances the information infrastructure through common interoperable standards and access to open networks. It also maximizes benefits of e-commerce by developing awareness and skills, encouraging widespread Small-Medium-Enterprise adoption, and ensuring participation and use by all countries;

*   finding alternative ways of improving trading partner trust relationships rather than relying on trading partner agreements; and

*   developing and designing a partnering charter (as in a trading partner relationship contract) which emphasizes trading partner trust behaviours in relation to e-commerce business operations.

The partnering charter (enclosed in the appendix) was developed by Siemens NZ and is a document which sets out mutually agreed objectives. The partnering charter is not a complex, unintelligible legal document, but is simply an agreement between the interested parties setting out mechanisms, procedures, and expectations of each trading partner towards the other, in clear, concise, and understandable terms. Partnering is a process of team building and mutual goal setting, where both trading parties are able to appreciate and understand the legitimate business aspirations of the other. Through this understanding they act appropriately for mutual benefit. The partnering charter is an evolving document modified and adjusted to suit the changing cultural, business, or political environments. Most fundamentally, it is an agreement based on trust.

Limitations of the Study

Despite the acknowledged importance of trust, current scholarly inquiry on the topic has been limited in two ways. First, little academic research exists that attempts to empirically document the factors affecting trust in trading relationships (Dyer and Chu, 2000; Hosmer, 1995; Sako, 1998). By and large, most IS research emphasizes information technology, IOS's, and their relative and competitive advantages. At the time when this study was initiated, no study was found that attempted to develop a theoretical framework of antecedent trust factors influencing business-to-business e-commerce participation on the Internet. Second, past research did not systematically distinguish trust from its related behaviours such as competence, reliability, predictability, commitment, and cooperation. Trust itself can be seen as a very complex and multi-dimensional construct and there have been numerous attempts to define and conceptualize it, its antecedents, and outcomes (Lewis and Weigert, 1985; McKnight et al., 1998; Wehmeyer et al., 2001).

The findings of this study may be constrained by the research context, i.e., dyadic relationships. Although, eight uni-directional dyads (organizations) were examined in this study, it cannot be regarded holistically (i.e., the results may not be generalizable), even though the evidence of the study contributed to key findings and interesting patterns in trading partner relationship management within an e-commerce environment. However, the researcher believes that many of the findings in this study have wider applicability. For example, competence trust and its correlation to economic benefits can be applied to many other organizations using e-commerce applications. Likewise, the issues or risks relating to trading partner trust (relational risks) can have broad applicability in most powerful trading partner relationships.

This study took a micro-perspective of inter-organizational trust. It was not intended to examine other aspects of e-commerce such as adoption process, types of e-commerce applications, cultural dimensions, or the size of organizations applying e-commerce. The study was restricted only to dyadic organizations involved in business-to-business e-commerce located in Melbourne (Australia) and Wellington (New Zealand) regions. It is possible that given different levels of social capital in different regions of the world, some of the results of this study may not be globally generalizable. Furthermore, this research examined only a subset of the possible characteristics and behaviours between trust and its antecedents, consequences, and moderating variables.

Future Research Directions

Future research should take a more extensive approach to cover all possible positive and negative characteristics and behaviours of trust in e-commerce participation. Though our findings supported the general theoretical framework, it is also possible that a different sequence of relationships setting similar to all cross-sectional studies longitudinal research can further enhance or refute the empirical findings. In addition, the dynamic and constantly changing context of the e-commerce environment may affect the nature of inter-organizational trust in the future. Therefore, longitudinal studies will probably be the research method of choice for understanding the role and nature of trust in e-commerce participation.

Since this study was primarily exploratory in nature and focused on identifying and examining the importance of trust behaviours within dyadic relationships in e-commerce participation, future research should address at greater length how this model could be used to explain inter-organizational trust at a wider scale. An abstract model incorporating many theories was developed for this study, as it was intended to be an exploratory study in nature. The next step is to examine the constructs in this model in greater depth by applying the most recent literature. For example, the constructs in this study could be improved to include more detailed measures, and it could be tested extensively (using a survey).

This chapter discussed the model of inter-organizational trust within bi-directional dyads in e-commerce participation leading to contributions to theory and practice. In addition, practical guidelines were given for businesses and e-commerce adopters. Finally, we discussed the limitations of this study and directions and recommendations for future research as part of a longitudinal study.

References

Achrol, R.S. (1997). Changes in the theory of inter-organizational relationships in marketing: Toward a network paradigm, *Journal of Academy of Marketing Science*, (25:1), 56-71.

Aggarwal, R. & Zabihollah, R. (1994). Introduction to EDI controls, *IS Audit & Control Journal*, (11), 64-68.

Ambrose, P.J. & Johnston, G.J. (1997). A trust based model of buying behavior in electronic retailing, *Association for Information Systems, Americas Conference in Information Systems*, Baltimore, Maryland, August 14-16, 263-265.

Anderson, E. & Weitz, B.A. (1989). Determinants of continuity in conventional channel dyads, *Marketing Science*, (8:4), 310-323.

Anderson, J.C. & Narus, J.A. (1984). A model of the distributor's perspective of distributor-manufacturer working relationships, *Journal of Marketing*, (48), Fall, 62-74.

Anderson, J.C. & Narus, J.A. (1990). A model of distributor firm and manufacturer firm working partnerships, *Journal of Marketing*, (54), January, 42-58.

Applegate, L.M., Holsapple, C.W., Kalakota, R., Radermacher, F.J., & Whinston, A.B. (1996). Electronic commerce: Building blocks of new business opportunity, *Journal of Organizational Computing and Electronic Commerce*, (6:1), 1-10.

Arunachalam, V. (1997). Electronic data interchange: Issues in adoption and management, *Information Resources Management Journal*, (10:2), Spring, 22-31.

Baker, S. (2000). Getting the most from your intranet and extranet strategies, *Journal of Business Strategy*, July/August, 40-43.

Bakos, J.Y. (1991). Information links and electronic marketplaces: The role of the inter-organizational information systems in vertical markets, *Journal of Management Information System*, (8: 2), 31-52.

Bakos, Y. (1998). The emerging role of electronic marketplaces on the Internet, *Communications of the ACM*, (41:8), August, 35-48.

Banerjee, S. & Golhar, D.Y. (1994). Electronic data interchange: Characteristics of users and nonusers, *Information and Management*, (26), 65-74.

Barclay, D.W. (1991). Interdependent conflict in organizational buying: The impact of organizational context, *Journal of Marketing Research*, May, (28: 2), 145-160.

Barney, J.B. & Hansen, M.H. (1994). Trustworthiness as a source of competitive advantage, *Strategic Management Journal*, (15), 175-216.

Barrett, M.I. (1999). Challenges of EDI adoption for electronic trading in the London insurance market, *European Journal of Information Systems*, (8), 1-15.

Benbasat, I., Goldstein, D.K., & Mead, M. (1987). The case research strategy in studies of information systems, *MIS Quarterly*, September, 368-383.

Benjamin, R.I., de Long, D.W., & Morton, S. (1990). Electronic data interchange: How much competitive advantage? *Long Range Planning*, (23: 1), 29-40.

Bensaou, M. & Venkatraman, N. (1995). Configurations of inter-organizational relationships: A comparison between US and Japanese automakers, *Management Science*, (41: 9), 1471-1492.

Bensaou, M. & Venkataman, N. (1996). Inter-organizational relationships and information technology: a conceptual synthesis and a research framework, *European Journal of Information Systems*, (5), 84-91.

Berry, L.L. (1999). *Discovering the Soul of Service: The Nine Drivers of Sustainable Business Success*, New York: Free Press.

Bhimani, A. (1996). Securing the commercial Internet, *Communications of the ACM*, (39:6), June, 29-35.

Bigley, G.A. & Pearce, J.L. (1998). Straining for shared meaning in organization science: Problems of trust and distrust, *Academy of Management Review*, (23: 3), 405-421.

Blau, P. (1964). *Exchange and Power in Social Life*, New York: Wiley.

Blois, K.J. (1999). Trust in business to business relationships: An evaluation of its status, *Journal of Management Studies*, (36: 2), 197.

Bonoma, T.V. (1985). Case research in marketing: Opportunities, problems, and a process, *Journal of Marketing Research*, (22), 199-208.

Bradach, J.L. & Eccles, R.G. (1989). Prices, authority and trust: From ideal type to plural forms, *Annual Review of Sociology*, (15:1), 97-118.

Brensen, M. (1996). An organizational perspective on changing buyer-supplier relations: A critical review of the evidence, *Organization Articles*, (3:1), 121-146.

Bromiley, P. & Cummings, L.L. (1992). Transaction costs in organizations with trust, Working Paper 28, Strategic Management Research Center, University of Minnesota, Minneapolis.

Brynjolfsson, E. & Smith, M. (2000). Frictionless commerce? A comparison of Internet and conventional retailers, *Management Science*, (46: 4), 563-585.

Burns, D.C. (1991). EDI security and controls - Internal audit needs to examine low electronic data interchange alters the effectiveness of internal controls designed for processing transactions the traditional way, *Bank Management*, 27-31.

Business Management. (1999). Converting risk aversion – Trust: The Quantum Competitive Advantage.

Caelli, W., Longley, D., & Shain, M. (1991). *Information Security Handbook*, M Stockton Press.

Caelli, W.J. (1997). Information security in electronic commerce, *PACIS, The Pacific Asia Conference on Information Systems, Brisbane, Queensland*, Australia, April, 1-5.

Campbell, R.P. (1993). Developing security for EDI, *EDI World*, April 40-45.

Carney, M. (1998). The competitiveness of networked production: The role of trust and asset specificity, *Journal of Management Studies*, (35:4), July, 457-480.

Carr, J. (1991). Electronic Data Interchange-Security Risk or Not? *Computers and Security*, Elsevier Science Publishers Ltd, (10), 69-72.

Caruso, D. (1995). *New York Times*, Monday, June 24th.

Cash, J.I. & Konsynski, B.R. (1985). IS redraws competitive boundaries, *Harvard Business Review*, (63: 2), 134-142.

Cavalli, A. (1995). Electronic commerce over the Internet and the increasing need for security, *TradeWave*, Dec 8.

CERT, C.E.R.T.C.C. (2000). *Infosec Outlook*, 1.

Chan, S. & Davis, T. (2000). Partnering on extranets for strategic advantage, *Information Systems Management*, (17:1), 58-64.

Chellappa, R.K. (2001). Working Paper, ebizlab, Los Angeles.

Chellappa, R.K. & Pavlou, P.A. (2001). Perceived information security, financial liability and consumer trust in E-commerce transactions, *Journal of Management Information Systems*.

Chiles, T.H. & McMackin, J.F. (1996). Integrating variable risk preferences, trust, and transaction costs economics, *Academy of Management Review*, (21:1), 73-99.

Cisco Solutions. (1998). *Internet Commerce Solution – Creating Competitive Advantage in the New Internet Economy*.

Clarke, R. (1997). Promises and Threats in Electronic Commerce, http://www.anu.edu.au/people/Roger.Clarke/EC/Quantum.html.

Clemons, E.K., Reddi, S.P., & Row, M.C. (1993). The impact of information technology on the organization of economic activity: The move of the middle hypothesis, *Journal of Management Information Systems*, (10:2), Fall, 9-35.

Coleman, A. (1994). EDI: An application often without a responsible owner, *IS Audit & Control Journal*, (11), 14-16.

Coleman, J.S. (1990). *Foundations of Social Theory*, Cambridge, MA, Belknap Press.

CommerceNet. (1997). Barriers & inhibitors to the widespread adoption of Internet commerce, CommerceNet Research Report #97-05, April 1997.

Cooper, M.C. & Gardner, J. (1993). Building good business relationships – More than just partnering or strategic alliances? *International Journal of Physical Distribution and Logistics Management*, (23: 6), 14-26.

Coopers and Lybrand Consultants. (1992). Electronic data interchange in Australia: A Coopers & Lybrand Survey of Australia's Top 1,000 Companies, April.

Coutu, D.L. (1998). Organization – trust in virtual teams, *Harvard Business Review*, May-June 1998, 20-21.

Covello, V.T. & Merkhofer, M.W. (1994). *Risk Assessment Methods*, Plenum Press, New York.

Cox, B. & Ghoneim, S. (1996). Drivers and barriers to adopting EDI: A sector analysis of UK industry, *European Journal of Information Systems*, (5), 24-33.

Cummings, L.L. & Bromiley, P. (1996). The organizational trust inventory (OTI): Development and validation. In R. M. Kramer & T. R. Tyler (Eds.), *Trust in Organizations: Frontiers of Theory and Research*, Sage Publications, Thousand Oaks, CA, 302-220.

Das, T.K. & Teng, B.-S. (1996). Risk types and inter-firm alliance structures, *Journal of Management Studies*, (33: 4), 827-843.

Das, T.K. & Teng, B.-S. (1998). Between trust and control: Developing confidence in partner cooperation in alliances, *Academy of Management Review*, (23: 3), 491-512.

Dearing, B. (1990). The strategic benefits of EDI, *The Journal of Business Strategy*, (11: 1), January/February, 4-6.

Deutsch, M. (1958). The Effect of motivational orientation upon trust and suspicion, *Human Relations*.

Di Turi, B.B. (1993). Security for EDIFACT messages, *Computers and Security*, (12: 5), August, 447-455.

Doney, P.M. & Cannon, J.P. (1997). An examination of the nature of trust in buyer-seller relationships, *Journal of Marketing*, April, 35-51.

Dosdale, T. (1994). Security in EDIFACT systems, *Computer Communications*, (17: 7), July, 532-537.

Dow, R., Napolitano, L., & Pusateri, M. (1998). *The Trust Imperative: The Competitive Advantage of Trust-based Business Relationships*, National Account Management Association, Chicago, Illinois, 1-14. http://ownbey.net/james/notes/4433/trsut-imperative-1.html

Drummond, R. (1995) Safe and secure electronic commerce, *Network Computing*, December, (7:19), 116-121.

Dwyer, R.F., Schurr, P. H., & Oh, S. (1987) Developing buyer-seller relationships, *Journal of Marketing*, (51), 11-27.

Dyer, J.H. & Chu, W.C. (2000) The determinants of trust in supplier automaker relationships in the U.S., Japan and Korea, *Journal of International Business Studies*, (31: 2), 259-185.

EDICA. (1990). EDI Control Guide- Make your Business More Competitive, *EDI Council of Australia and EDP Auditors Association*.

Emmelhainz, M.A. (1990). *A Total Management Guide*, NCC Blackwell.

Fearson, C. & Phillip, G. (1998). Self-assessment as a means of measuring strategic and operational benefits from EDI: The development of a conceptual framework, *European Journal of Information Systems*, (7), 5-16.

Forrester Research. (1999). *Corporate Electronic Commerce Prediction.* http://thestandard.net/metrics/display/0,1283,865,00.htm

Fukuyama, F. (1995). *Trust: The Social Virtues and the Creation of Prosperity*, Free Press.

Fung, R. & Lee, M. (1999). Trust in electronic commerce: Exploring antecedents factors, *Proceedings of the 5th Americas Conference on Information Systems*, 517-519.

Gabarro, J. (1987). *The Dynamics of Taking Charge*. Boston: Harvard
Business School Press.

Galliers, R. D. (1992). Choosing information systems research approaches, In
R. D. Galliers (Ed.), *Issues, Methods and Practical Guidelines*,
Blackwell Scientific Publications: Oxford.

Gambetta, D. (1988). *Trust: Making and Breaking Cooperative Relations*,
Basil Blackwell, New York.

Ganesan, S. (1994). Determinants of long-term orientation in buyer-seller
relationships, *Journal of Marketing*, (58), April, 1-19.

Gentry, D. J. (1994). Selecting financial EDI software, *TMA Journal*, 40-45.

Geyskens, I., Steenkamp, J.B., & Kumar, N. (1998). Generalizations about
trust in marketing channel relationships using meta-analysis, *International Journal in Marketing*, (15), 223-248.

Ghosh, S. (1998). Making business sense of the Internet, *Harvard Business
Review*, March-April, 126-135.

Giaglis, G.M., Paul, R.J., & Doukidis, G.I. (1998). Dynamic modelling to
assess the business value of electronic commerce, electronic commerce
in the information society, *Eleventh International Bled Electronic
Commerce Conference*, Bled, Slovenia, June 8-10, 57-73.

Gorriz, C.M. (1999). *Electronic Commerce and Trust on the Internet*, http://
/www.future.sri.com/bip/bulletin/Dldesc/2080.shtml

Granovetter, M. (1985). Economic action and social structure: The problem of
embeddedness, *American Journal of Sociology*, (91: 3).

Griffith, D.A., Hu, M.Y., & Ryans, J.K., Jr. (2000). Process standardization across intra and inter cultural relationships, *Journal of International Business Studies*, (31:2), 303-324.

Gulati, R. (1995). Does familiarity breed trust? The implications of repeated ties for contractual choice in alliances, *Academy of Management Journal*, (38:1), 85-112.

Handy, C. (1995). Trust and the virtual organization, *Harvard Business Review*, 73, 3, May-June, 40-50.

Hart, P., & Saunders, C. (1997). Power and trust: Critical factors in the adoption and use of Electronic Data Interchange, *Organization Science*, (8:1), 23-42.

Hart, P., & Saunders, C. (1998). Emerging electronic partnerships: Antecedents and dimensions of EDI use from the supplier's perspective, *Journal of Management Information Systems*, (14: 4), Spring, 87-111.

Heck & Ribbers. (1999). The adoption and impact of EDI in Dutch SMEs, *The Hawaii International Conference in Information Systems*.

Heil, G., Bennis, W., & Stephens, D. (2000). *Douglas McGregor, Revisited: Managing the Human Side of the Enterprise*, John Wiley and Sons.

Helper, S. (1991). How much has really changed between U.S automakers and their suppliers? *Sloan Management Review*, (32: 4), 15-28.

Henderson, J.C. (1990). Plugging into strategic partnerships: The critical IS connection, *Sloan Management Review*, (31: 3), 7-13.

Hicks, M. (1999). *A matter of trust, PC Week Online*, http://www.techserver.com/noframes/story/0,2294,500179918500236906-501168697-0,00.html

Hill, C.W.L. (1990). Cooperation, opportunism, and the invisible hand: Implication for transaction cost theory, *Academy of Management Review*, (15), 500-513.

Hoffman, D.L., & Novak, T.P. (1995). *Marketing in Hypermedia Computer-Mediated Environments: Conceptual Foundations*, Revised July 11, (http://www2000.ogsm.vanderbilt.edu/cmepapaer.revision.july11.1995/cmepaper.html)

Hoffman, D.L., Kalsbeek, W.D., & Novak, T.P. (1996). Internet and Web use in the US, *Communication of the ACM*, (39:12), 36-46.

Hoffman, D.L., Novak, T.P., & Peralta, M. (1999). Association for computing machinery, *Communications of the ACM*, (42), 80-85.

Hoffman, N.P. (2000). An examination of the sustainable competitive advantage concept: Past, present and future, *Academy Marketing Science Review*, Online, http://www.amsreview.org/amsrev/theory/hoffman00-04.html

Hosmer, L.T. (1995). Trust: The connecting link between organizational theory and philosophical ethics, *Academic Management Review*, (20:2), 379-403.

Hruska, S. (1995). The Internet: A strategic backbone for EDI? *EDI Forum*, (8: 4), 83-85.

Iacovou, C.L., Benbasat, I., & Dexter, A.S. (1995). Electronic data interchange and small organizations: Adoption and impact of technology, *MIS Quarterly*, (19: 4), 465-485.

Jamieson, R. (1994). Electronic commerce - Meeting the audit challenge, *IS Audit and Control Journal*, (11), 10-12.

Jamieson, R. (1996). Auditing and electronic commerce, *EDI Forum*, Perth, Western Australia.

Jamieson, R. & Low, G. (1991). Controlling EDI technology - The impact of electronic data interchange technology on security and audit, *Computer Control Quarterly*, (9:9), 16-29.

Jarvenpaa, S.L., Tractinsky, N., & Vitale, M. (2000). Consumer trust in an Internet store, Information technology and management, *Information Technology and Management*, (1), 45-71.

Jevans, D. (1999). Extranets rev up EDI, *ECOM World*, www.ecomworld.com/html/entrpriz/020199-3.htm

Johnston, H.R. & Vitale, M.R. (1988). Creating competitive advantage with inter-organizational information systems, *MIS Quarterly*, (12:2), 153-165.

Kalakota, R. (1996). Manager's guide to electronic commerce: Addison-Wesley, Spring, (forthcoming) previewed in E. Burns (Ed.), *Defining Electronic Commerce: EDICAST*, Issue 28, February/March. 5.

Kalakota, R. & Robinson, M. (2001). *E-Business 2.0: Roadmap of Success*, Addison Wesley.

Kalakota, R. & Whinston, A.B. (1996). *Frontiers of Electronic Commerce*, Addison-Wesley Publishing Company.

Keen, P.G.W. (1997). Are you ready for the 'trust' economy? *Computer World*, April (21:31), 16- 80.

Keen, P.G.W. (1999). *Electronic Commerce and the Concept of Trust*, http://wwww/peterleen.com/ecr1.htm

Keen, P.G.W. (1999). *Electronic Commerce: How Fast, How Soon?* http://strategis.ic.gc.ca/SSG/mi06348e.html

Keen, P.G.W. (2000). Ensuring E-trust, *Computerworld*, March 13.

Kipnis, D. (1996). *Trust and Technology, Trust in Organizations: Frontiers of Theory and Research*, Sage Publications, Thousand Oaks, CA, 39-50.

Klein, H.K. & Myers, M.D. (1996). *The evaluation of interpretative research in information systems*, Department of Management Science and Information Systems, University of Auckland, 1-44.

Kozak, R.A. & Cohen, D.H. (1997). Distributor-supplier partnering relationships: A case in trust, *Journal of Business Research*, (39), 33-38.

Kramer, R.M. & Tyler, T.R. (1996). Whither trust. In R. M. Kramer & T. R. Tyler (Eds.), *Trust in Organizations: Frontiers of Theory and Research*, Sage Publications, Thousand Oaks, CA.

Kraut, R. & Steinfield, C. (1994). *The Effect of Networks on Buyer-Seller Relationships: Implications for the National Information Infrastructure*, http://commtechlab.msu.edu/humans/steinfield/TPRC94.html

Kumar, K., van Dissel, H.G., & Baielli, P. (1998). The merchant of Prato – revisited: Toward a third rationality of information system, *MIS Quarterly*, June.

Kumar, N. (1996). The power of trust in manufacturer-retailer relationships, *Harvard Business Review*, Nov-Dec, 92-106.

Kumar, N., Scheer, L. K., & Steenkamp, J. E. M. (1995). The effects of supplier fairness on vulnerable resellers, *Journal of Marketing Research*, (33), 54-65.

Langfield-Smith, K., & Greenwood, M. R. (1998). Developing co-operative buyer-supplier relationships: A case study of Toyota, *Journal of Management Studies*, (35: 3), 331-353.

Lee, M.K.O., & Turban, E. (2001). A trust model for consumer Internet shopping, *International Journal of Electronic Commerce*, (6:1), 75-92.

Lemos, R. (2001). Volume 2001, MSNBC.com

Lepkowska-White, E., Swaminathan, V., & Rao, B. (1999). Browsers or buyers in cyberspace. An investigation of factors influencing electronic exchange, *Journal of Computer Mediated Communications*, JCMC, (5: 2). http://www.ascusc.org/jcmc/vol5/issue2/swaminathan.htm.

Leverick, F. & Cooper, R. (1998). Partnerships in the motor industry: Opportunities and risks for suppliers, *Long Range Planning*, (31:1), 72-81.

Lewicki, R. J. & Bunker, B. B. (1996). Developing and maintaining trust in work relationships. In R. M. Kramer & T. R. Tyler (Eds.), *Trust in Organizations: Frontiers of Theory and Research*, Sage Publications, Thousand Oaks, CA, 114-139.

Lewis, J. D., & Weigert, A. (1985). Trust as a social reality, *Social Forces*, (63:4), 967-983.

Liddy, C. (1996). Commercial security on the Internet, *Information Management and Computer Security*, (4:1), 47-49.

Lim, S.B. & Jamieson, R. (1994). EDI risks, security and control: An Australian survey. *Fifth Australian Conference on Information Systems*.

Mackay, D., & Rosier, M. (1996). Measuring organizational benefits of EDI diffusion, *International Journal of Physical Distribution & Logistics Management*, (26:10), 60-78.

Macneil, R. (1980). *The New Social Contract*, New Haven, CT, Yale University Press.

Malone, T.W., Yates, J., & Benjamin, R.I (1987). Electronic markets and electronic hierarchies, *Communication of the ACM*, (30:6), 484-497.

Marcella, A. J., Jr. & Chan, S. (1993). *EDI Security, Control and Audit*, Artech House Inc.

Marcella, A. J., Stone, L., & Sampias, W.J. (1998). *Electronic Commerce: Control Issues for Securing Virtual Enterprises*, The Institute of Internal Auditors.

Massetti, B. & Zmud, R. (1995). Measuring the extent of EDI usage in complex organizations: Strategies and illustrative examples, *MIS Quarterly*, (20:3), 331-345.

Mayer, R.C., Davis, J.H., & Schoorman, F.D. (1995). An integrative model of organizational trust, *Academy of Management Review*, (20:3), 709-734.

McAllister, D.J. (1995). Affect and cognition-based trust as foundations for interpersonal cooperation in organizations, *Academy of Management Journal*, (38:1), 24-59.

Mcknight, H.D., Cummings, L.L., & Chervany, N.L. (1998). Managers as initiators of trust: An exchange relationship framework for understanding managerial trustworthy behavior, *Academy of Management Review*, (23:3), 513-530.

McWilliams, B. (2000). News for 02/03/00 12.30 pm ET Internet News Radio (Online Radio) http://stream.internet.com/Content/inr2000203.ram.

Menkus, B. (1992). Understanding EDI security issues, *Computers & Security*, October, (11:6), 525-528.

Meyer, K.D. (1998). Believing what you can't see, the importance of trust in business and technology, *Managing Office Technology*.

Miles, M.B. & Huberman, A.M. (1994). Qualitative data analysis, *An Expanded Sourcebook (2nd ed.)*, SAGE Publications.

Miles, R.E. & Snow, C.C. (1992). Causes of failure in network organizations, *California Management Review*, 53-72.

Miller, D. & Shamsie, J. (1999). Strategic responses to three kinds of uncertainty: Product line simplicity at the Hollywood Film Studios, *Journal of Management*, (25:1), 97-116.

Mishra, A.K. (1996). Organizational responses to crisis – The centrality of trust. In R. M. Kramer & T. R. Tyler (Eds.), *Trust in Organizations: Frontiers of Theory and Research*, Thousand Oaks, CA: Sage Publication, 261-287.

Miyazaki, A.D. & Fernandez, A. (2000). *Journal of Public Policy & Marketing*, (19), 54-61.

Mohr, J. & Spekman, R. (1994). Characteristics of partnership success: Partnership attributes, communication behavior, and conflict resolution techniques, *Strategic Management Journal*, (15), 135-152.

Moorman, R., Zaltman, G., & Deshpande, R. (1992). Relationships between providers and users in market research relationships: The dynamics of trust within and between organizations, *Journal of Marketing Research*, (29), 314-329.

Moorman, R., Zaltman, G., & Deshpande, R. (1993) Factors affecting trust in market research relationships, *Journal of Marketing*, (57), January, 81-101.

Morgan, R.M., & Hunt, S.D. (1994). The commitment-trust theory of relationship marketing, *Journal of Marketing*, (58), 20-38.

Mukhopadyay, T., Kekre, S., & Kalathur, S. (1995). Business value of information technology: A study of electronic data interchange, *MIS Quarterly*, (19:2), 137-156.

Muller, N.J. (1998). How the Internet is breaking down barriers to EDI, Communications management, *Information Systems Management*, Summer, 78-81.

Myers, M. (1994). Quality in qualitative research in information systems, *5th Australian Conference in Information Systems*, 763-766.

Nath, R., Akmanligil, M., Hjelm, K., Sakaguch, T., & Schultz, M. (1998). Electronic commerce and the Internet: Issues, problems and perspectives, *International Journal of Information Management*, (18: 2), 91-101.

Neuman, S. (1994). *Strategic Information Systems: Competition through Information Technologies*, Macmillan College Publishing Company, New York.

New York Times. (2000). Study predicts huge growth in business to business Web sector, Bloomberg News, June 27th.

Norlan and Norton Institute, KPMG. (1999). *Electronic Commerce – The Future is Here.*

O'Brien, E.C. (1995). Is trust a calculable asset in the firms? *Business Strategy Review*, Winter, 39-54.

O'Hara-Devereaux, M. & Johansen, B. (1984). *Global Work: Bridging Distance, Culture, and Time*, Jossey-Bass Publishers, San Francisco.

Oliver, W.G. (1990). Markets, bureaucracies and clans, *Administrative Science Quarterly*, (25), 129-144.

Orlikowski, W.J., & Baroudi, J.J. (1991). Studying information technology in organizations: Research approaches and assumptions, *Information Systems Research*, (2), 1-28.

Palmer, J.W., Bailey, J.P., & Faraj, S. (2000). The role of intermediaries in the development of trust on the WWW: The use and prominence of trusted third parties and privacy statements, *Journal of Computer Mediated Communication*, (5:3), Online.

Parker, D.B. (1995). A new framework for information security to avoid information anarchy, *IFIP*, 155-164.

Parkhe, A. (1998). Understanding trust in international alliances, *Journal of World Business*, (33:3), 219-240.

Pavlou, P.A. & Ba, S. (2000). Does online reputation matter? An empirical investigation of reputation and trust in online auction markets, *Proceedings of the 6ᵗʰ Americas Conference in Information Systems*, Long Beach, Carlifornia.

Pfeffer, J. & Salancik, G.R. (1978). *The External Control of Organizations: A Resource Dependency Perspective*, Harper & Row Publishers.

Picard, G. (1992). *EDI for managers and auditors*, NCC Blackwell, 1-167.

Premkumar, G., & Ramamurthy, K. (1995). The role of inter-organizational and organizational factors on the decision mode for adoption of inter-organizational systems, *Decision Sciences*, (26: 3), 303-336.

Premkumar, G., Ramamurthy, K., & Crum, M. (1997). Determinants of EDI adoption in the transportation industry, *European Journal of Information Systems*, (6), 107-121.

Premkumar, G., Ramamurthy, K., & Nilakanta, S. (1994). Implementation of EDI - An innovation diffusion perspective, *Journal of Management Information Systems*, (11:2), 157-186.

Provan, K.G. & Gassenheimer, J.B. (1994). Supplier commitment in relational contract exchanges with buyers: A study of inter-organizational dependence and exercised power, *Journal of Management Studies,* (31), 55-68.

Pugh, D.S., Hickson, D.J., Hinnings, C.R., & Turner, C. (1968). Dimensions of organizational structure, *Administrative Science Quarterly*, (13), 65-105.

Pyle, R. (1996). Electronic commerce and the Internet, *Communications of the ACM*, June, (39: 6), 23.

Raman, D. (1996). Cyber assisted business – EDI as the backbone of electronic commerce, *EDI-TIE*.

Ratnasingam, P. (1998). Internet based EDI trust and security, *Information Management and Computers Security*, (6:1), 33-39.

Ratnasingam, P. (2000). The influence of power among trading partners in business to business electronic commerce, *Internet Research*, (1), 56-62.

Ratnasingam, P. & Klein, S. (2001). Perceived benefits of Inter-Organizational-Trust in E-commerce participation – A Case Study in the Telecommunication Industry, *American Conference in Information Systems*, Boston, Massachusetts, Aug 3-5th.

Ratnasingam, P., & Kumar, K. (2000). The importance of inter-organizational-trust in business to business E-commerce participation – Case Studies in New Zealand, *11th Australian Conference in Information Systems* – Dec 6th –8th, Brisbane, Australia, 71-84.

Ratnasingam, P. & Kumar, K. (2000). Trading partner trust in E-Commerce participation, *21st International Conference in Information Systems (ICIS)*, Dec 10th – 13th, Brisbane, Australia, 544-552.

Ratnasingam, P., & Pavlou, P. (2002). Technology trust: The next value creator in B2B electronic commerce, *Information Resources Management Association Conference*, Seattle, Washington, May 19th – 22nd, pp. 889-894.

Ratnasingam, P. & Pavlou, P. (2003). Technology trust in Internet-based interorganizational electronic commerce, *Journal of Electronic Commerce in Organizations*, v 1, no 1, pp. 17-41, (Jan-Mar), Inaugural Issue.

Rayport, J.E. & Jaworski, B.J. (2001). *E-Commerce*, McGraw-Hill/Irwin.

Rayport, J.F & Sviokla, J.J. (1994). Managing in the marketspace, *Harvard Business Review*, November-December, 141-150.

Reekers, N. & Smithson, S. (1996). The role of EDI in inter-organizational coordination in the European automotive industry, *European Journal of Information Systems*, (5), 120-130.

Riggins, F.J. & Mukhopadhyay, T. (1999). Overcoming EDI adoption and implementation risks, *International Journal of Electronic Commerce*, (3: 4), 103-123.

Riggins, F.J. & Rhee, H.S. (1998). Toward a unified view of electronic commerce, *Communications of the ACM*, (41: 10), 88-95.

Ring, P.S. & Van de Ven, A.H. (1992). Structuring cooperative relationships between organizations, *Strategic Management Journal*, (13), 483-498.

Ring, P.S. & Van de Ven, A.H. (1994). Developing processes of cooperative inter-organizational relationships, *Academy of Management Review*, (19), 90-118.

Rochester, J.B. (1989). The strategic value of EDI, *IS Analyzer*, Volume 7.

Rousseau, D.M., Sitkin, S.B., Burt, R.S., & Camerer, C. (1998). Not so different after all: A cross-discipline view of trust, *The Academy of Management Review*, (23: 3), 393-404.

Sabel, C.F. (1993). Studied trust – Building new forms of cooperation in a volatile economy, *Human Relations*, (49: 9), 1133-1171.

Sabo, D. (1997). Industry pulse: Electronic commerce barriers survey results, *ITAA*.

Sako, M. (1992). *Prices, Quality and Trust: Inter-firm relations in Britain & Japan*. New York, Cambridge University Press.

Sako, M. (1998). Does trust improve business performance? In C. M. Lane, & Bachmann (Eds.), *Trust Within and Between Organizations – Conceptual Issues and Empirical Applications*, Oxford University Press.

Sako, M. & Helper, S. (1998). Determinants of trust in supplier relations: Evidence from the automotive industry in Japan and the United States, *Journal of Economic Behavior and Organization*, (34), 387-417.

Sarkar, M.B., Butler, B., & Steinfeld. (1995). Intermediaries and cybermediaries: A continuing role for mediating players in the electronic marketplace, *Journal of Computer Mediated Communication*, (1: 3).

Saunders, C. & Clark, S. (1992). EDI adoption and implementation: A focus on inter-organizational linkages, *Information Resources Management Journal*, (5: 1), 9-19.

Scala, S. & McGrath, R. Jr. (1993). Advantages and disadvantages of electronic data interchange: An industry perspective, *Information & Management*, (25: 2), 85-91.

Schurr, P.H. & Ozanne, J.L. (1985). Influence on exchange processes: Buyer's perception of a seller's trustworthiness and bargaining toughness, *Journal of Consumer Research*, (11), March, 939-953.

Senn, J.A. (1996). Capitalizing on electronic commerce – The role of the Internet in electronic markets, getting on board the Internet, *Information Systems Management*, Summer, 15-25.

Senn, J.A. (1998). Expanding the reach of electronic commerce – The Internet EDI alternative, *Information Systems Management*, Summer, 7-15.

Senn, J.A. (2000). Business to business E-commerce, *Information Systems Management*, Spring 2000, 23-32.

Shanks, G.., Rouse, A., & Arnott, D. (1993). A review of approaches to research and scholarship in information systems, Working Paper Series, Monash University, Department of Information Systems.

Shapiro, D., Sheppard, B.H., & Cheraskin, L. (1992). Business on a hand-shake, *The Negotiation Journal*, October, 365-378.

Sharp, D.E. (1998). Extranets: Borderless Internet/intranet networking, stra-tegic directions, *Information Systems Management*, Summer, 31-35.

Shaw, R.B. (1997). *Trust in Balance – Building Successful Organizations on Results, Integrity, and Concern*, Jossey-Bass Publishers.

Silverman, D. (1998). Qualitative research meanings and practices? *Information Systems Journal*, (8), 3-20.

Sitkin, S.B. & Pablo, A.L. (1992). Re-conceptualizing the determinants of risk behavior, *Academy of Management Review*, (17: 1), 9-38.

Smeltzer, L. (1997). The meaning and origin of trust in buyer-seller relation-ships, *International Journal of Purchasing and Materials Manage-ment*, Tempe, Winter, (33: 1), 40-48.

Smith, J.B. & Barclay, D.W. (1997). The effects of organizational differences and trust on the effectiveness of selling partner relationships, *Journal of Marketing*, (61), 3-21.

Speier, C., Harvey, M., & Palmer, J. (1998). *Journal of World Business*, (33), 263-276.

Steinfield, C., Kraut, R., & Plummer, A. (1998). The impact of interorganizational networks on buyer-seller relationships, *Journal of Computer Mediated Communications* (JCMC) (1: 3), 1-16. (http://111.ascusc.org/jcmc/vol1/issue3/steinfld.html)

Stewart, D.W., Pavlou, P.A., & Ward, S. (2001). In E. Zillman (Ed.), *Media Effects: Advances in Theory and Research*, Elbaum, Hillsdale, N.J.

Stewart, T.R. (1998). *Selected E-business issues – Perspectives on business in Cyberspace*, Deloitte Touche Tohmatsu, September, 1-26.

Storrosten, M. (1998). Barriers to electronic commerce, *European Multimedia, Microprocessor Systems and Electronic Commerce Conference and Exhibition*, Bordeaux, France.

Sullivan, J., Peterson, R.B., Kameda, N., & Shimada, J. (1981). The relationship between conflict resolution approaches and trust – A cross cultural study, *Academy of Management Journal*, (24:4), 803-815.

Sydow, J. (1998). Understanding the constitution of Inter-Organizational-Trust, In C. Lane & R. Bachmann (Eds.), *Trust within and between Organizations, Conceptual Issues and Empirical Applications*.

Tallon, P.P., Kraemer, K.L., & Gurbaxani, V. (2000). Executives perceptions of the business value of information technology: A process-oriented approach, *Journal of Management Information Systems* (16), 145-173.

Tan, Y.-H. & Thoen, W. (1998). Towards a generic model of trust for electronic commerce, *International Journal of Electronic Commerce* (3), 65-81.

Thompson, J.D. (1967). *Organizations in Action*, New York: McGraw-Hill.

Turban, E., Lee, J., King, D., & Chung, H.M. (2000). *Electronic Commerce: A Managerial Perspective*, Prentice Hall Inc.

Van de Ven, A.H. & Ferry, D.L. (1976). On the nature, formation and maintenance of relations among organizations, *Academy of Management Review*, (1: 4), 24-36.

Van de Ven, A.H. & Ferry, D.L. (1980). *Measuring and Assessing Organizations*, New York, John Wiley & Sons.

Veliyath & Fitzgerald, E. (2000). Firms capabilities, business strategies, customer preferences, and hypercompetitive arenas, *Competitiveness Review*, (10:1), 56-83.

Venkatraman, N. & Zaheer, A. (1990). Electronic integration and strategic advantage: A quasi-experimental study in the insurance industry, *Information Systems Research*, (1:4), 377-393.

Vijayasarathy, L.R. & Robey, D. (1997). The effect of EDI on market channel relationship in retailing, *Information and Management*, (33), 73-86.

Walsham. (1993). *Interpreting Information Systems in Organizations*, Wiley, Chichester, England.

Walsham, G. (1995). The emergence of interpretivism in information systems research, *Information System Research*, (6: 4), 376-394.

Walton, S.V. (1997). The relationship between EDI and supplier reliability, *International Journal of Purchasing and Materials Management*, (33:3), 30-35.

Wanninger, L.A. (1998). Profitable electronic commerce – Framework, examples, trends, *Eleventh International Bled Electronic Commerce Conference*, Bled, Slovenia, June 8-10, 3-27.

Webb, J. & Gile, C. (2001). Reversing the value chain, *Journal of Business Strategy*, (22), 13-17.

Webster, J. (1995). Networks of collaboration or conflict? Electronic data interchange and power in the supply chain, *Journal of Strategic Information Systems*, (4), 1, 31-42.

Webster, J. F. E. (1992). The changing role of marketing in the corporation, *Journal of Marketing*, (56), October, 1-17.

Wehmeyer, K., Riemer, K., & Schneider, B. (2001). Role and trust in inter-organizational systems, *8th Research Symposium on Emerging Electronic Markets*, forthcoming.

Wicks, A.C., Berman, S.L., & Jones, T.M. (1999). The structure of optimal trust: Moral and strategic implications, *Academy Management Review*, (24: 1), 99-116.

Wigand, R.T. & Benjamin, R.I. (1997). Electronic commerce: Effects on electronic markets, *Journal of Computer-mediated Communication*, (1:3). http://jcmc.huji.ac.il/vol.1/issue3/wigand.html

Williamson, O.E. (1975). *Markets and Hierarchies, Analysis and Anti-trust Implications*, The Free Press, New York.

Williamson, O.E. (1985). *The Economic Institutions of Capitalism – Firms, Markets, Relational Contracting*, The Free Press – A Division of Macmillan, Inc.

Williamson, O. E. (1991). Calculativeness, trust and economic organization, *Journal of Law and Economics*, (26), (April) 453-386.

Williamson, O.E. (1993). Opportunism and its critics, *Managerial and Decision Economics*, (14), 97-107.

WTO. (1998). Electronic commerce and the role of the WTO. *WTO Secretariat*, March.http://www.wto.org/wto/new/press96.htm

Yin, R. K. (1984). *Case Study Research: Design and Methods*, Sage Publications.

Yin, R. K. (1989). *Case Study Research: Design and Methods*, Sage Publications.

Yin, R.K. (1994). *Case Study Research: Design and Methods (2nd ed.)*, Sage Publications, Thousand Oaks, CA.

Yovovic, B.G. (1996). Trust among partners foundation of success, *Advertising Age's Business Marketing*, (81: 6), 12-13.

Zaheer, A. & Venkatraman, N. (1995). Relational governance as an inter-organizational strategy: An empirical test of the role of trust in economic exchange, *Strategic Management Journal*, (16), 373-392.

Zaheer, A., McEvily, B., & Perrone, V. (1998). Does trust matter? Exploring the effects of interorganizational and interpersonal trust on performance, *Organization Science*, (9:2), 141-159.

Zucker, L.G. (1986). Production of trust: Institutional sources of economic structure: 1840-1920. In B.Staw & L.Cummings (Eds.), *Research in Organizational Behaviour,* (8), 53-111.

Zwass, V. (1996). Electronic commerce: Structures and issues, *International Journal of Electronic Commerce*, Fall, (1:1), 3-23.

Appendix

SEMI-STRUCTURED QUESTIONNAIRE DESIGN

The semi-structured questionnaire includes four sections:

Section 1

Section 1 consists of three parts. The objective of the first part was to obtain background (demographic) information about the organizations. The questions included: type of organization, size, number of trading partners, types of products, and the type of e-commerce technology/application adopted. The second part of Section 1 examines factors that motivate the organization to adopt e-commerce and determines antecedent trust behaviours in trading partners. A total of 18 items were applied to evaluate different types of trading partner trust. Competence trust was examined using two antecedent trust behaviour questions that relate to trading partners' ability, skills, competence, and their level of dependence. Predictability trust was examined with four antecedent trust behavioural questions about consistent trading partners' behavioural patterns leading to knowledge gained and enabling other trading partners to make predictions. Finally, goodwill trust was examined with twelve antecedent trust behavioural questions about care, concern, open communication, training, education, and commitment, and other factors leading to long-term trading partner relationships.

The third part of Section 1 examined factors relating to trust and security-based mechanisms in e-commerce. A total of 20 items identified trust and security-based mechanisms in organizations. Confidentiality was examined with two questions about privacy (encryption mechanisms and firewalls). Integrity was examined with five questions about data accuracy and completeness. Authentication was examined with one question about formal user log-on procedures. Non-repudiation was examined with one question about acknowledgement procedures. Access controls were examined with two questions about authorization mechanisms and network access controls. Availability was examined with one question about segregation of duties. Finally, best business practices were examined with seven questions about audit involvement, risk analysis, top management commitment, and contingency procedures.

Section 2

The object of Section 2 was to examine the organizations' perceived benefits in participation in e-commerce. Perceived benefits derived from both trading partner trust relationships and trust and security-based mechanisms in e-commerce were examined. A total of 13 items were used to examine perceived benefits from four different categories. Perceived direct benefits (or economic benefits) were examined using four questions about tangible economic benefits derived from cost savings. Perceived indirect benefits were examined with four questions about productivity, profitability, and competitive advantage. Perceived relationship-related benefits were examined with three questions about trading partner satisfaction (i.e., improved communication, cooperation, and commitment). Finally, perceived strategic benefits (or symbolic benefits) were examined with two questions about organizations' image, reputation, and long-term investments.

Section 3

Section 3 examines the organizations' perceived risks of e-commerce. Perceived risks derived from both trading partner trust relationships and trust and security-based mechanisms in e-commerce were examined. A total of 25 items was applied to examine perceived risks from three different categories. Perceived technology performance-related risks were examined using seven questions about the e-commerce technology. Perceived relational risks were examined using eight questions about trading partners' uncertainties, unreliability, and signs of opportunistic behaviours. Finally, perceived general risks were examined using ten questions about poor business practices such as a lack of proper standards, written policies, and procedures.

Section 4

Section 4 examines an organization's extent of e-commerce participation. E-commerce participation was examined from two different perspectives. A total of 11 questions was applied to examine e-commerce participation from two different categories. E-commerce performance was examined with four questions about the intensity, volume, and dollar value of the e-commerce transactions. Trading partner trust relationship development was examined with seven questions about cooperation, communication, commitment, and reputation.

For each of these questions, respondents were asked to indicate their impact level using likert scales (as in Low (0-3), Medium (4-6), and High (7-10)). They indicated explanations and reasons on their responses. Participants provided examples and evidence for each question even if their responses were negative. This helped develop causal links and provided richer explanations. Hence, by consistently applying the semi-structured questionnaire across all cases, reliability of the data was achieved and led to meaningful generalizations and conclusions about the importance of different types of trading partner trust in e-commerce participation. These conclusions yielded consistent results that supported and confirmed the predictions, refuted the predictions, or produced mixed results that made explaining and reasoning difficult at times.

Construct	Sub-Concepts	Definition	Evaluation Pointers & Instrumentation
Trust in Trading Partners	*Competence Trust*	Ability, skills, knowledge and competence of trading partners to perform business to business e-commerce correctly and completely	Examines competence trading partner trust via two items. How, why, to what extent, and in what situations (provide evidence and examples)
	Predictability Trust	Consistent behaviours of trading partners that allow another trading partner to make predictions and judgements due to past experiences	Examines predictability trading partner trust via four items. How, why, to what extent, and in what situations (provide evidence, and examples)
	Goodwill Trust	Care, concern, honesty, and benevolence shown by trading partners that allows the other trading partner to further invest in their trading partner relationship	Examines goodwill trading partner trust via twelve items. How, why, to what extent, and in what situations (provide evidence, and examples)
Technology Trust Mechanisms in E-Commerce	*Confidentiality*	Protection of e-commerce transactions and message content against unauthorized reading, copying, or disclosure	Examines confidentiality mechanisms via two items. How, why, to what extent, and in what situations (provide evidence, and examples)
	Integrity	Accuracy and assurance that e-commerce transactions have not been altered or deleted	Examines integrity mechanisms via five items. How, why, to what extent, and in what situations (provide evidence, and examples)
	Authentication	Quality of being authoritative, valid, true, genuine, worthy of acceptance or belief by reason of conformity to the fact that reality is present	Examines authentication mechanisms via one item. How, why, to what extent, and in what situations (provide evidence, and examples)
	Non-Repudiation	Originator of e-commerce transactions cannot deny receiving or sending that transaction	Examines non-repudiation mechanisms via one item. How, why, to what extent, and in what situations (provide evidence, and examples)
	Access Controls	Protection of e-commerce transactions against weaknesses in the transmission media and protection of the sender against internal fraud or manipulation	Examines access control mechanisms via two items. How, why, to what extent, and in what situations (provide evidence, and examples)

	Availability	Assurance that passes or conveys e-commerce transactions without interruption by providing authorized users with e-commerce systems	Examines availability mechanisms via one item. How, why, to what extent, and in what situations (provide evidence, and examples)
	Best Business Practices	Policies, procedures and standards that ensure smooth functioning of e-commerce	Examines best business practices via seven items How, why, to what extent, and in what situations (provide evidence, and examples)
Perceived Benefits of E-Commerce	Perceived Economic Benefits of E-Commerce	Benefits derived from direct savings in costs and time	Examines direct perceived benefits via four items How, why, to what extent, and in what situations (provide evidence, and examples)
	Perceived Relationship-Related Benefits of E-Commerce	Benefits derived from closer trading partner relationship such as open communications, information sharing, cooperation, and commitment	Examines human related perceived benefits via three items. How, why, to what extent, and in what situations (provide evidence, and examples)
	Perceived Strategic Benefits of E-Commerce	Benefits derived from long-term business investments and improved reputation of the organization	Examines strategic perceived benefits via two items. How, why, to what extent, and in what situations (provide evidence, and examples)
Perceived Risks of E-Commerce	Perceived Technology Performance Related Risks of E-Commerce	Risks derived from misuse of the e-commerce technology, integrity, viruses, confidentiality, unauthorized access, availability	Examines technology related perceived risks via seven items. How, why, to what extent, and in what situations (provide evidence, and examples)
	Perceived Relational Risks of E-Commerce	Risks derived from trading partner's behaviour, such as opportunistic behaviour, conflict, power	Examines people related perceived risks via eight items. How, why, to what extent, and in what situations (provide evidence, and examples)
	Perceived General Risks of E-Commerce	Risks derived from environmental risks, standards and audit policies	Examines general perceived risks via ten items. How, why, to what extent, and in what situations (provide evidence, and examples)
Outcomes of E-Commerce Participation	Extent of E-Commerce Performance	Intensity, volume and dollar value of the business transactions	Examines e-commerce performance via four items. How, why, to what extent, and in what situations (provide evidence, and examples)
	Extent of Trading Partner Trust Development	Trading partner relationship development	Examines mutual satisfaction in trading partner relationships via seven items. How, why, to what extent, and in what situations (provide evidence, and examples)

CASE STUDY QUESTIONNAIRE

Date:

To whom it may concern

Dear Sirs

Re: A Study of Inter-organizational Trust in Business-to-Business E-Commerce Participation

The purpose of this study is to examine the impact of inter-organizational trust in e-commerce participation. E-commerce participation refers to the extent an organization adopts, integrates, or implements business-to-business e-commerce. Inter-organizational trust is actually interpersonal trust; hence it also refers to trading partner trust. We aim to examine how and why inter-organizational trust (or trading partner trust) influences the perception of benefits and risks in e-commerce, thus leading to the extent of e-commerce participation. We believe that you will find it interesting and useful to participate in this study. It is our hope that this knowledge will help increase business to business e-commerce participation.

The questionnaire consists of four sections.

Section 1

This section seeks to obtain background (demographic) information about your organization. We seek information relating to factors that motivated your organization to adopt e-commerce and determine antecedent trust behaviours relating to trading partner relationships, trust, and security-based mechanisms in e-commerce participation.

Section 2

This section seeks information about your organization's perception of benefits in e-commerce participation (that is, perceived benefits derived from both trading partner relationships and technology trust mechanisms in e-commerce).

Section 3

This section seeks information about your organization's perception of risks in e-commerce participation (that is, perceived risks derived from both trading partner relationships and technology trust mechanisms in e-commerce).

Section 4

This section seeks information about your organization's extent of e-commerce participation.

Confidentiality

All responses will be kept in its strictest confidence. No individuals or organizations will be named in any outputs, nor will demographic information be revealed, such that the individual organizations can be identified. When the results of this study are published, it will be impossible to identify specific individuals or organizations, unless prior permission was received.

Summary Results

We will send a summary of the results to all organizations that participate in this study. The summary will provide conclusions related to the extent that inter-organizational trust impacts perceived benefits and risks, thus leading to business to business e-commerce participation. We truly appreciate the time and effort you have put into this study. Your response will be of considerable help to this study.

Thank You
Ms. Pauline Ratnasingam

Figure 1: Conceptual model of trading partner trust in e-commerce participation

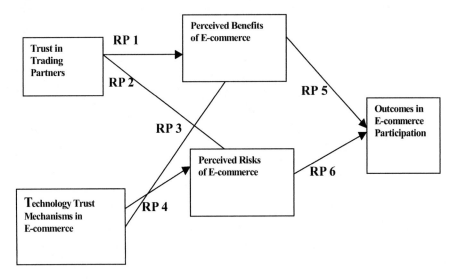

RESEARCH TOPIC: THE IMPORTANCE OF INTER-ORGANIZATIONAL TRUST IN E-COMMERCE PARTICIPATION

Research Question: How and why does inter-organizational trust (trading partner trust) influence the perception of benefits and risks in business-to-business e-commerce, thus leading to the extent of its participation (adoption and integration)?

Section 1

A)   Demographic Section

    1.   Name of your organization?

    2.   Your job title?

    3.   What is your organization's reach? (Local, regional, national, or global?)

4. What is the size of your organization – (Large or small-medium-enterprise?)

5. Type of industry and sector your organization is involved in (Public or private?)

6. What is your organization's product line?

7. What is the main role of your organization? (Buyer, seller, manufacturer, or supplier?)

8. Who is responsible for implementing e-commerce and is involved in e-commerce operations in your organization?

9. What types of business transactions are actively supported by e-commerce in your organization?

10. What types of e-commerce technologies/applications did your organization implement or will be implementing?

11. How many trading partners does your organization have?

12. How did your organization choose its trading partners?

13. How long has your organization been trading with these trading partners?

14. How do you maintain your trading partners (Renewal of contracts)?

15. What other measures are used?

B) Trading Partner Trust

Trading Partner Trust – refers to the expectation that one trading partner will abide to the trading contract, is honest, and will act in a way not to take advantage of other trading partners. Trading partner trust is categorized as low, moderate, and high.

Please indicate your organization's reflections on behavioural characteristics relating to trading partner trust relationships. If yes, how, why, and in what situations do you relate these behaviours to trading partner trust (please provide examples and evidence)? Are there other trust behaviours that your organization faces in e-commerce participation?

Competence Trading Partner Trust

1. Trading partner's ability, skills, and level of competence in business to business e-commerce operations.

2. Trading partner depends on your organization.

Predictability Trading Partner Trust

3. Trading partner's consistent behaviour in business interactions.

4. Trading partner's reliability in keeping business promises.

5. Trading partner's adherence to policies, terms of contract, and trading partner agreements.

6. Predictability of your trading partner.

Goodwill Trading Partner Trust

7. Trading partner's willingness to share information and provide support relating to e-commerce adoption.

8. Trading partner demonstrates care and concern in important decisions.

9. Trading partner is committed to business arrangements and exhibits cooperation.

10. Positive feelings towards your trading partner.

11. Long-term trading relationships with your trading partner.

12. Your organization is willing to put in more effort and invest in your trading partner relationships.

13. Trading partner is honest in providing information and shows accuracy in meeting deadlines

14. Trading partner behaviour in a situation of conflict and handling discrepancies. Does your organization feel anger, frustration, resentment, or hostility towards your trading partner?

15. Trading partner in a situation of pressure or imbalance of power.

16. Trading partner considers security concerns.

17. Trading partner is the driving force for adopting e-commerce.

18. There are explicit agreements with the trading partners regarding roles and responsibilities.

     How do you maintain your trading partner relationships? Is it short-term or long-term? What do you look for? How, why, and in what situations?

     On a scale of 10 what would you rate the level of trading partner trust? (Low = 0-3, Medium = 4-6, High = 7-10)

     What did you rate the level of trading partner trust to be? How, why, and in what situations?

     Are there other antecedent trust behaviours your organization perceived in your trading partners?

C) Technology Trust Mechanisms in E-commerce

    Technology trust mechanisms in e-commerce refer to trust assurances such as confidence in the security protection services provided by e-commerce technologies.

Please indicate if your organization has adopted the following technology trust mechanisms in e-commerce. If yes, how, why, and in what situations were they implemented (please provide examples, evidence)? Are there any other technology trust mechanisms that your organization has implemented?

Confidentiality

1.   Firewalls

2.   Encryption mechanisms

Integrity

3.   System integrity tests and audits

4.   Sequence numbers in messages

5.   Application controls

6.   Accounting controls

7.   Web seal assurances

Authentication

8.   Formal log-on procedures (user-ID's and passwords)

Non-repudiation

9.   Message receipt confirmations and acknowledgments

10. Digital signatures

Access Control

11. Network access controls

12. Authorization mechanisms

Availability

13.   Segregation of duties

Best Business Practices

14.   Top management commitment

15.   Standards (industry and universal) and polici

16.   Trading Partner Agreement

17.   Audit check

18.   Training and education of staff

19.   Risk analysis and audit involvement

20.   Contingency procedures

On a scale of 1-10, how would you rate the level of trust and security mechanisms in e-commerce? (Low = 0-3, Medium = 4-6, High = 7-10)

What did you rate the level of trust and security-based mechanisms in e-commerce?

How, why, and in what situations?

Are there any other trust and security mechanisms in e-commerce your organization has implemented?

How does trading partner trust influence the perception of trust and security-based mechanisms in e-commerce?

Section 2: Perceived Benefits in E-commerce Participation

Perceived benefits refer to gains that your organization may receive from adopting e-commerce. The perceived benefits are derived from both your trading partner relationships and from the e-commerce technology. Perceived benefits are categorized as direct (economic), indirect, relationship-related, and strategic benefits.

Please indicate if your organization faces the following benefits. If yes, how, why, and in what situations do you relate to the perceived benefits (please provide examples, evidence)? Are there any other perceived benefits your organization faces? How does trading partner trust influence the perception of benefits in your organization?

Perceived Economic Benefits
1.   Reduced operation, transaction, and administrative costs

2.   Reduced error rates and improved accuracy of information exchanged

3.   Faster response to orders creating reduced lead time

4.   Reduced inventory levels and optimized supply chain

5.   Improved customer service and product quality

6.   Improved productivity, improved profitability, and increased sales

7.   Gaining competitive advantage

8.   Sharing of risks with your trading partner

Perceived Relationship-related Benefits
9.   Improved communication and cooperation with your trading partners

10.   Sharing of information that is accurate, timely, speedy, complete, and relevant

11.   Increased level of commitment with your trading partners

Perceived Strategic Benefits
12.   Improved organizational image and reputation

13.   Increased long-term investments and continued trading partner relation-
      ships

      On a scale of 10, how would you rate the level of perceived benefits in e-
      commerce? (Low = 0-3, Medium = 4-6, High = 7-10)

      What is the impact of these perceived benefits as a result of trading partner
      trust and technology trust mechanisms in your organization?

      What did you rate the level of perceived benefits to be?

      How, why, and in what situations?

      Are there any other perceived benefits in e-commerce your organization
      faces?

Section 3: Perceived Risks in E-commerce Participation

Perceived risks refer to barriers and obstacles your organization faces as
a result of adopting e-commerce. Perceived risks are derived from both trading
partner relationships and from the e-commerce technology. Perceived risks are
categorized as technology performance-related risks, relational risks, and
general risks.

Please indicate if your organization faces the following perceived risks. If
yes, how, why, and in what situations do you relate to these perceived risks
(please provide examples, evidence)? Are there any other perceived risks that
your organization faces? How does trading partner trust influence the perception of risks in your organization?

Perceived Technology Performance-related Risks
1.   Compatibility problems with hardware and software

2.   Infrastructure and initial implementation costs

3.   Confidentiality concerns due to viruses

4. Lack of adequate accounting controls

5. Internal security error (lack of integrity, as in delayed and inaccurate messages)

6. Complexity in operating business transaction

7. Uncertainties (task and environment)

Perceived Relational Risks
8. Trading partner reluctance to change

9. Lack of training, knowledge, and awareness

10. Poor reputation of trading partner

11. Trading partner demonstrating a conflicting attitude

12. Lack of trust in your trading partner

13. Trading partner demonstrating opportunistic behaviours

14. Partnership uncertainty

Perceived General Risks
15. Lack of security in your trading partner's system

16. Difficulty in identifying or quantifying costs and benefits

17. Repudiation

18. Authenticity of your trading partner

19. Availability of technology

20. Lack of a standard infrastructure (for data and payments)

21. Lack of government policies

22. Poor business practices

On a scale of 10 how would you rate the level of perceived risks in e-commerce to be? (Low = 0-3, Medium = 4-6, High = 7-10)

What is the impact of these perceived risks as a result of trading partner trust and technology trust mechanisms in your organization?

What did you rate the level of perceived risks in e-commerce to be?

How, why, and in what situations?

Are there any other perceived risks your organization faces?

Section 4: Outcomes in E-commerce Participation

Outcomes in e-commerce participation refers to the extent your organization has adopted e-commerce. Participation in e-commerce is categorized as performance in e-commerce and the extent of mutual satisfaction your organization has with its trading partners.

Please reflect on your organization's extent of e-commerce participation. If yes, how, why, and in what situations do you relate to e-commerce participation (please provide examples and evidence)? Are there any other factors that your organization faces which contribute to e-commerce participation?

Extent of E-commerce Performance
1. How important is e-commerce for your organization?

2. What percentage of your business involves the use of e-commerce?

3. What is the annual monetary value of e-commerce transactions in NZ$?

4. What is the annual number of e-commerce transactions?

On a scale of 10, how would rate the extent of e-commerce performance in your organization? (Low = 0-3, Medium = 4-6, High = 7-10)

What did you rank the extent of e-commerce performance in your organization?

How, why, and in what situations?

Are there any other performance factors relating to e-commerce your organization has achieved?

How does trading partner trust influence the perception of e-commerce performance?

How do perceived benefits impact e-commerce performance?

How do perceived risks impact e-commerce performance?

Extent of Trading Partner Trust Relationships Development

5.   The trading partner will continue to be a major source of revenue for us.

6.   Has the number of trading partners increased?

7.   Do you perceive your organization to engage in long-term business investments with your trading partner?

8.   Do you perceive an increase in the level of open communications in your trading partner?

9.   Do you perceive an increase in the level of cooperation in your trading partner?

10.   Do you perceive an increase in the level of commitment in your trading partner?

11.   Has the reputation of your organization increased as a result of your trading partner?

On a scale of 10, how would you rate the extent of satisfaction in your trading partner relationships? (Low = 0-3, Medium = 4-6, High = 7-10)

What did you rate the level of satisfaction in your trading partner relationships to be?

How, why, and in what situations?

Are there other factors relating to trading partner satisfaction that your organization experienced?

How does trading partner trust influence the perception of satisfaction in your trading partner relationships?

How do perceived benefits influence the perception of satisfaction in your trading partner relationships?

How do perceived risks influence the perception of satisfaction in your trading partner relationships?

CUSTOMER CONTRACT - PARTNERING FOR SUCCESS

Introduction

Sadly, relationships with our customers are often characterized by mistrust, poor communication, and adversity. Complex and onerous contracts are developed between the parties; the negotiation process is often long and arduous, setting a negative tone for the on-going relationship. Ultimately, contracts are there to protect each party from the misdemeanors of the other; they are conceived and written from a perspective of worst case scenario, and they are by definition not conducive to a cooperative relationship.

This paper seeks to identify a mechanism to restore trust and cooperation as well as business and cultural alignment between the parties.

Concept

The concept is simply partnering. The key to success is turning this nebulous concept into something tangible and meaningful for both parties and providing a basis for the continuing relationship.

Partnering is a process of team building and mutual goal setting where both parties are able to appreciate and understand the legitimate business aspiration of the other and through this understanding act appropriately for mutual benefit.

The Agreement

Key to the partnering concept is the *"Partnering Charter."* The Partnering Charter is a jointly developed document setting out mutually agreed upon objectives. The partnering charter is not a legal document, it is not complex, it is not unintelligible; it is simply an agreement between the interested parties setting out the mechanisms, procedures, and expectations of each party towards the other, in clear, concise, and understandable terms.

The partnering charter is an evolving document being modified and adjusted to suit the changing cultural, business, or political environments. Most fundamentally and overriding is that it is an agreement based on trust.

Creating the Charter

Perhaps even more valuable than the Charter is the process of creating it. Both parties work together to develop the document, and through these discussions an opportunity for relationship building and better understanding of mutual needs is provided.

Principles of a Partnering Charter

A charter will encompass the key needs of each party, specifically:

- Commitment – Partnering agreements are only effective with the buy-in of top management stakeholders.

- Equity – Both parties must recognize and appreciate the legitimate business aspirations of the other and work towards assisting their partner to achieving their objectives.

- Trust – Contracts are about suspicion, Charters are about trust—not only to write about trust but to implement the relationship and maintain it through communication. The creation of a Partnering Charter should be a positive and educational experience for both parties.

- Mutual Goals or Objectives – Generally contracts are written with the interest of one party in precedence. The Charter is based on reciprocal benefits and shared interests.

- On-going Evaluation – The Partnering Charter provides a mechanism for parties to measure their performance and voice legitimate concerns if or when commitments are not met. The Partnering Charter is a living document and will be constantly reviewed and modified

- Communications – Partnering agreements are an opportunity to bring together management stakeholders on a regular basis to evaluate the progress and the efficacy of the current agreement.

- Conflict Resolution -- Serious issues can be addressed early and corrections made before relationships break down and contracts are imposed.

Partnership Charter Clauses

The following are some generic clauses that could form part of a bi-lateral Partnership Charter:

Siemens Unilateral Commitments

- On-going development – We will keep you up to date with new products and solutions

- Education – We will train your staff to operate our products effectively

- Accuracy – Information provided will be accurate and honest, no hype, no misleading narrative

Customer Unilateral Commitments

- No surprises – If there is a problem we will tell you first

- Strategic planning – We will keep you informed of our business planning and future direction

- Forecasting – We will assist you to deliver on time by providing forecasting information

Reciprocal Agreements

- We are accountable – We take whole and total responsibility, no blaming third parties and no excuses.

- Honesty and Integrity – We are ethical business partners

- We keep our promises – What we say is what we do

- Confidentiality – If it's secret we will keep it that way

- Commitments – Verbal commitments are binding on both parties

The Process

One party would initiate the Partnering Charter, generally at senior management level and most effectively through a short presentation. Assuming broad agreement is reached, a follow-up or alignment meeting would be arranged to select a working group to develop the partnering plan.

A partnering workshop will be scheduled where both parties would prepare for the workshop with draft clauses that they wish to include in the Charter. It is recommended that such a workshop be administered by an external facilitator.

The outcome of the workshop will be the Partnering Charter encompassing at a minimum the elements already explored above.

Conclusion

The Partnering Charter can be used as a mechanism to enhance existing relationships or initiate new ones. In the typical vendor-customer relationship, the customer holds the power and therefore controls the relationship. The Partnership contract subtlely redresses the balance back towards the vendor and at the same time will be perceived by our customers as a proactive measure to improve our business process.

Good business is built primarily and fundamentally on good people relationships. The partnering charter provides a mechanism to establish and maintain such relationships.

About the Author

Pauline Ratnasingam, Ph.D, Assistant Professor of MIS, University of Vermont (USA), School of Business Administration, offers her perspective on her dissertation research titled "Inter-organizational Trust in Business to Business Electronic Commerce." Pauline Ratnasingam received her Bachelor's in Computing (Information Systems) and Honors in Information Systems from Monash University, Melbourne, Australia. She received her Ph.D from Erasmus University, Rotterdam School of Management, The Netherlands. In 1999, she was selected to participate in the Ernst & Young International Conference in Information Systems (ICIS) Doctoral Consortium, North Carolina, USA. She has presented papers at the ICIS 2000 conference at Brisbane, Australia, and the Information Resources Management Association (IRMA 2002) international conference at Seattle, Washington. She has lectured on the topics of Project Management, Management of Information Systems, and Electronic Commerce in Australia, New Zealand, Europe, and America. She is an associate member of the Association of Information Systems, and is a member of the Information Resources Management Association and Academy of Management. Her research interests include Business Risk Management, Internet-based business-to-business E-commerce, Organizational Behaviour, Inter-Organizational Relationships, and Trust. She has published several articles related to these areas in national and international conferences and refereed journals. She has received a grant from the National Science Foundation to pursue her work on inter-organizational trust in business-to-business E-commerce.

Index

Journal of Electronic Commerce in Organizations (JECO)

The International Journal of Electronic Commerce in Modern Organizations

ISSN: 1539-2937
eISSN: 1539-2929
Subscription: Annual fee per volume (4 issues):
Individual US $85
Institutional US $185

Editor: Mehdi Khosrow-Pour, D.B.A.
Information Resources
Management Association, USA

Mission

The *Journal of Electronic Commerce in Organizations* is designed to provide comprehensive coverage and understanding of the social, cultural, organizational, and cognitive impacts of e-commerce technologies and advances on organizations around the world. These impacts can be viewed from the impacts of electronic commerce on consumer behavior, as well as the impact of e-commerce on organizational behavior, development, and management in organizations. The secondary objective of this publication is to expand the overall body of knowledge regarding the human aspects of electronic commerce technologies and utilization in modern organizations, assisting researchers and practitioners to devise more effective systems for managing the human side of e-commerce.

Coverage

This publication includes topics related to electronic commerce as it relates to: Strategic Management, Management and Leadership, Organizational Behavior, Organizational Developement, Organizational Learning, Technologies and the Workplace, Employee Ethical Issues, Stress and Strain Impacts, Human Resources Management, Cultural Issues, Customer Behavior, Customer Relationships, National Work Force, Political Issues, and all other related issues that impact the overall utilization and management of electronic commerce technologies in modern organizations.

For subscription information, contact:

Idea Group Publishing
701 E Chocolate Ave., Ste 200
Hershey PA 17033-1240, USA
cust@idea-group.com
URL: www-idea-group.com

For paper submission information:

Dr. Mehdi Khosrow-Pour
Information Resources Management
Association
jeco@idea-group.com